that's a good
QUESTION

that's a good QUESTION

Pondering 24 of God's Surprising Questions

BarbaraJo Tripp Bowers

As Psalm 45:1 says, "My heart is stirred by a noble theme. . ." so the reading of BarbaraJo Tripp Bowers' book has stirred my heart with a noble theme. *That's a Good Question* is not only a well-crafted book of biblical insight for the hearts and minds of God's people today, but it is also an important and compelling offering of encouragement to untold numbers of people who are bewildered with life, bereft of encouragement, and bankrupt of hope.

BarbaraJo's careful adherence to Scripture and the important questions God asks helps the reader to take a deeper dive into God's Word, be immersed in the profound revealing of God's heart, and be comforted with the good news only Jesus can offer. Her focus on Jesus' passion to save us and give us life through His merits and sacrifice alone are indeed the sum and substance of her book.

This book is suitable for quiet nights of private contemplation as well as a text for classroom Bible study, and even a primer for healthy theological lecture and debate. It breathes fresh air into the deep places of people's lives where they work, play, live, love, think, and feel.

Reading Ms. Tripp Bowers' zest to bring the good news of Jesus into people's hearts allows the eye to take in what many ears and hearts have already received. Ferociously committed to God's Word, her thoughts, wisdom, and teaching offer sound, orthodox theology as well as contemporary insights that many will find applicable to their lives and situations.

Not only is *That's a Good Question* a must-read for pastors, Sunday School and Bible class teachers and leaders in the church, but it should have a place in the homes of all followers of Jesus who seek to grow closer to Him and deeper in their faith. For years to come this book will remain a resource for teaching, an encouragement in contemplation, and a beacon light of hope amid the dark tomes of new age philosophies and non-biblical theologies.

Pastor Bill Yonker
Senior Pastor, Immanuel Lutheran Church
East Dundee, Illinois

That's a Good Question is a book that will stimulate thought and meditation. BarbaraJo provides impetus for careful consideration of the questions God asks. God's questions, of course, do not spring from a knowledge deficit. He knows all. But His questions prompt contemplation of ourselves, more importantly of Him. You will enjoy ways this book will spur you to meditate on the goodness of God and His wisdom in dealing with His people. It is a book you can dip into randomly to be confronted with human neediness and overwhelmed with the grace and mercy of God.

DR. TEDD TRIPP
Pastor Emeritus, Author, Conference Speaker

That's a Good Question
Pondering 24 of God's Surprising Questions

Copyright © 2022, BarbaraJo Tripp Bowers

ISBNS:
Paper: 978-1-63342-108-0
ePub : 978-1-63342-109-7
Mobi: 978-1-63342-111-0

Unless otherwise noted, Scripture quotations are from the ESV® (The English Standard Version®), copyright © 2001 by Crossway, a publishing ministry of Good News Publishers. Used by permission. All rights reserved.

No part of this publication may be reproduced, or stored in a retrieval system, or transmitted, in any form or by any means, mechanical, electronic, photocopying, recording or otherwise, without the prior permission of Shepherd Press.

Cover design and typeset by www.greatwriting.org

Printed in Colombia

Shepherd Press
P.O. Box 24
Wapwallopen, PA 18660
www.shepherdpress.com

Table of Contents

Foreword 10
"Where have you come from and where are you going?" 14
"Adam, where are you?" 20
"Where is Abel your brother?" 26
"Who is this that darkens counsel by words without knowledge?" 32
"What is your name?" 40
"What is that in your hand?" 48
"Whom shall I send, and who will go for us?" 56
"Have I not commanded you?" 64
"How long will you grieve over Saul?" 72
"What are you doing here, Elijah?" 78
"Should I not pity Nineveh?" 86
"Do you want to be healed?" 94
"Do you see this woman?" 100
"Who was it that touched me?" 106
"Why are you discussing the fact that you have no bread?" ..112
"Why are you so afraid?" 118
"Who do you say that I am?" 126
"Do you want to go away as well?" 132
"Where are the nine?" 138
"So, could you not watch with me one hour?" 146
"Woman, why are you weeping?" 152
Children, do you have any fish? 160
"Do you love me?" 166
"Saul, Saul, why are you persecuting me?" 174
Conclusion 182
Afterword 186

Quoted biblical text occasionally rendered in italics is to reflect the author's emphasis.

"Now to Him who is able to keep you from stumbling and to present you blameless before the presence of his glory with great joy, to the only God, our Savior, through Jesus Christ our Lord, be glory, majesty, dominion, and authority, before all time and now and forever. Amen."
(Jude 24,25)

For my sixteen remarkable grandchildren, whom I cherish.

For George, who is my muse.

❖

Foreword

There are five questions I have advised parents to ask their children in moments where there have been relational or behavioral problems, and correction or discipline may be needed.

- What was going on? (Asking the child to recount the situation.)
- What did you do in response? (Asking the child to examine his behavior.)
- What were you thinking and feeling as you did it? (Asking the child to examine the heart behind the behavior.)
- Why did you do it, and what were you seeking accomplish? (Asking the child to examine his motives.)
- What was the result? (Asking the child to consider the consequences of his actions.)

I'm sure you noticed that none of these questions is asked in search for information. They are asked because these moments of correction and discipline provide an opportunity for something more than parental judgment and the meting out of punishment. They provide an opportunity for a parent to help the child examine his heart, the very thing children don't naturally do. As the connection is revealed between the thoughts and desires of his heart and his behavior, he is given the opportunity, not only to own his wrong behavior, but to admit that he has a deeper heart problem. As he begins to have insight into the condition of his heart, his is being made ready to hear the gospel of the grace of Jesus, who alone has the power to rescue us from us and transform our hearts.

If you want to be a tool of change in the hands of the Savior, you will be committed to asking good questions. There are three things to be said about this.

First, insightful people are not first the people who have the right answers. Insightful people are the people who ask the right questions, because you don't get the the right answers without the right questions.

Second, personal spiritual insight is the result of community. Sin blinds, and guess whom it blinds first? I have no difficulty at all seeing the sin of the people around me, but I can be blind to my own. I can't say that no one knows me better than I know myself, because spiritual blindness means that there will be pockets of inaccuracy in the way I look at myself. So, I need instruments of seeing in my life, who help me to see what I would not see if left to myself. (See Hebrews 3:12, 13.) Being an instrument of seeing means you lovingly and patiently ask questions of the person that he would not be able to ask himself.

The third thing to say about being an instrument of seeing by asking good questions is that, when you do this, you are following the way of your Heavenly Father. Your Bible is filled with moments when God asks just the right question of just the right person. He never does this in a search of information, because there is nothing in the universe that He does not know. He does this because He is not just a perfectly holy judge, but He is also a God of amazingly patient grace, who delights in giving His children heart- and life-changing insights. In His questions, His love is revealed. In His questions, His patience is seen. In His questions, His wisdom is highlighted. In His questions, His transforming grace operates. In His questions we have hope, because they tell us we are loved with a sturdy and patient love that our worst moments of rebellion and foolish behavior cannot destroy.

I love the book that you are about to read. I can honestly say that there is no book like this one, that studies the questions of God and applies them to your daily life. Come to this book with an open, humble, and willing heart, and, if you do, you will see yourself and see your Lord in ways that will change you.

I love the ending of the book of Jonah. It doesn't actually have an ending, because it ends with God asking stubborn and angry

Jonah a question. That question makes it very clear that Jonah can't outrun God's grace. After all of his running, pouting, and anger, God is still in a patient and perseverant pursuit of His prophet. You see, He will not let us go. He will pursue us with His questions of grace and He will do that until we are on the other side and His work of rescuing, forgiving, empowering, transforming, and delivering grace is done.

I love the glory of God's grace that shines in the pages of this book and I love the depth of gospel insights that splash across every page. But the thing that I love most about this book is that it will leave you loving your Lord more deeply and with a stronger hope in the transforming power of His love. So read slowly with an open heart, meditate on the insights here, and be thankful that the One asking these profound questions is, by grace, your Father forever.

PAUL DAVID TRIPP
Pastor, Author, and Conference Speaker
October, 2022

1

"Where have you come from and where are you going?"

GENESIS 16:8

And he said, "Hagar, servant of Sarai, where have you come from and where are you going?" She said, "I am fleeing from my mistress Sarai."

I first became interested in God's questions as I studied the life of Hagar, the slave girl who was owned by (and worked in the home of) Abraham and Sarah. Her story is recorded for us in Genesis chapter 16.

In Abraham's day, being without offspring was not just a disappointment, as it may be considered in our day. It was actually a disgrace, considered at times as a censure from God. To be without heirs was devastating. Sarah, Abraham's wife, who could not conceive children, approached her husband with the idea that they could achieve a family through Sarah's young housemaid, Hagar.

Hagar was probably one of the spoils of war—a captive. Slaves' opinions are not sought. They existed by the will, and to do the will, of their masters. Because Hagar was not consulted, and as a slave could not give free consent, she was, in effect, raped when her nearly one-hundred-year-old master had sexual relations with her in order to produce a child.

When Hagar became pregnant, predictably, there arose a problem between her and her mistress. Surely Hagar knew that she possessed within her body something Sarah would give *anything* to have—Abraham's child. Perhaps Hagar walked a little straighter, obeyed a little slower, smiled a smug grin now and then. However it manifested itself, Hagar became a little "uppity" for a servant. After all, wasn't she more valuable now? Sarah was not pleased. After all, Hagar was a *slave. Her* slave.

Sarah complained to Abraham. "She looked on me with contempt," was Sarah's lament. Abraham, the head of his family under God, could have mediated between the two women in his household. He should have been the "priest" in his home, a peacemaker. Instead, he washed his hands of the whole affair, perhaps impatient with what he considered women's squabbles.

So he told Sarah, "Your servant is in your power; do to her as you please"—it was not Abraham's finest hour.

The ESV euphemistically says that Sarah dealt harshly with Hagar. The NIV, with equal understatement, says that Sarah mistreated Hagar. Though we do not have the detailed account in Scripture of what really happened between Sarah and Hagar, it is clear that Sarah abused her; probably she beat her.

And Hagar ran away.

Really? What was Hagar thinking? Running away was surely an act of desperation. It was suicidal. She was running into the desert, where there was nothing that could sustain life, and much that could end it. Further, she was *pregnant*. She ran away in anger, and now she was in grave danger.

But, God loved Hagar. God cared for this Gentile slave girl. She had nothing. She was no one. She had no way to survive and no one would have mourned her death. Amazingly, God followed her into the desert. He is called in Genesis 16 "the *angel of the* Lord," a common phrase used in the Old Testament, and understood to be the preincarnate Christ. Theologians call His appearance a *theophany;* that is, an appearance of God in human form. God pursued Hagar into the desert. She could never have imagined the deep love of God. *Oh, the deep, deep love of Jesus!*

I was surprised to read that God addressed her with a *question*, a two-part question:

"Where have you come from and where are you going?"

Immediately, I stopped to contemplate this strange question. Strange, because I was well schooled in the omniscience of God. God knows everything about everything. There is absolutely nothing hidden from God. It follows that God never asks questions to gain information. He doesn't need to be informed.

God knew well where Hagar had come from, that she had run away from the home of Abraham and Sarah, and He knew that she had no idea where she was going. She *had* no place to go! So why the question?

Well, God, the Creator and Sustainer of everything there is, from the tiniest microscopic DNA to the expanse of galaxies, is

"Where have you come from and where are you going?"

the master teacher. All teachers throughout human history have derived their skill from Him.

> Thou only art the truth; all wisdom dwells in Thee,
> Thou source of every skill, eternal verity.[1]

God's questions inform the questions of all teachers throughout the ages. He doesn't ask questions to gain knowledge. Instead, He asks questions for the benefit of the person to whom He addresses the question. A penetrating question forces the person addressed to face what is really the truth. We call it a *rhetorical* question.

Human sin and weakness can cause one to deny the truth, to avoid it, to delude oneself. God's pointed questions force one to confront reality. It is part of God's gracious rescue of sinners.

Hagar was stopped dead in her tracks. She realized full on what she had done (Was it irreversible?) and the bleakness, even desperation, of her future. When she acknowledged her flight from her situation, God must have shocked her with the directive: "Return to your mistress and submit to her." Return? *Really?* Submit?

God followed this command with a prophecy of her future descendants. Yes, she would live and see grandchildren. She responded. "You, God, see me," expressed Hagar's understanding that God was fully aware of her suffering and had compassion on her.

Sadly, generations of Christian children misguidedly memorized the words, "You, God, see me," even sang about them. Unfortunately the application was a bit scary, a bit threatening, the idea being that God is looking down in judgment upon your activities. "Be careful what you do; God is looking." Of course God sees *everything,* but what a misunderstanding of these sweet words that comforted and encouraged Hagar!

Assured of God's tender love for her, Hagar obeyed His order for her to return to Sarah. How hard that must have been! I can imagine her steps were slow, her legs heavy as she trudged back to Sarah. It wouldn't be a happy reunion. She was going back to an angry mistress, and no runaway slaves were treated well upon their return.

---

1   Margaret Clarkson, *We Come O Christ, To Thee*

But with God's loving presence, Hagar—and I—and you—can face anything. You see, at the time I contemplated this bit of Bible history, I myself was going through a most difficult time of life following a painful divorce after a long-term marriage.

In the words of Ben Patterson, who through his book on suffering introduced me to this story, *God calls us to courage and responsibility in the face of suffering*. God assured Hagar during this desert meeting that He saw her. He knew and fully understood her suffering. But He still called her. Yes, she would live to be *His* servant to do His will.

"Where have you come from and where are you going?"

God asked it of me. Good question! I had four children in various stages of dependence upon me. I had responsibilities. I must not sulk in the desert of my despair. This beautiful story got me moving. I had to confront a long history of fear and anger which held me in bondage to people-pleasing. I had to admit that everything I faced was for my good and His glory. Ahead of me were responsibilities as well as great opportunities. I had to repent of my past failures and exercise faith for my future.

God still asks of wounded, rebellious, hopeless sinners, "Where have you come from and where are you going?" He gets our attention in order to bring us to repentance and heal all our brokenness. He who well knows where we came from invites us to recollect our journey in life. It's the beginning of repentance. He who intends to save us from ourselves, and all the demons who bully us, opens our eyes to see that we are traveling toward deeper and deeper darkness. And He opens our eyes to show us a better path, His plans for a glorious future redeemed by His blood, directed by His love.

This beautiful story of God's deliverance led me to contemplate other questions of God in Scripture. I found that there were quite lot of them, and, as I study them, I worship the Master Teacher.

"Where have you come from and where are you going?"

"Where have you come from and where are you going?"

For Further Thought

Psalm 136:1–9
Psalm 139:13–18
Romans 8:31–39
Ephesians 3:14–21
Hebrews 13:5,6

ND# 2

"Adam, where are you?"

GENESIS 3:9

But the L ord God called to the man and said to him, "Where are you?"

This is the very first question of God recorded in Scripture, and it is the most profound. It seems at first glance to be a simple question, but an examination of the situation renders the occasion of this question almost unthinkable. It is astonishing and disturbing.

The question is addressed to Adam, the first and only man, the male human being unique among all that God made. God created Adam on the sixth and final day of creation, His crowning achievement so to speak.

Further, in Genesis 1:26, we learn that God created man in His own image, after the likeness of God. Theologians have long debated just what that does and doesn't mean, but one thing is clear: man was profoundly different from all the rest of creation, and was peerless in his resemblance to God. The significance of the first man, Adam, to God and to the rest of the human race to follow, cannot be overstated.

Adam was given dominion over all creation. His was the broad and important task of naming all the plants and animals. His was the daily task of tending to the large and beautiful Garden of Eden. He was the original farmer, the first husbandman, and his vocation was given him by God, his Creator.

Adam would be the first husband, the first father. He was given the mandate to be fruitful and multiply and fill the earth with his progeny.

How could it be, then, that one day God called out in the Garden, "Adam, where are you?" Did God lose Adam? No, of course not. As we have previously stated, God always knows the answers to His questions before He asks them. He is omniscient. There is nothing He does not know. God did not misplace Adam!

Previously, Adam and God, as friends are known to do, walked and talked together daily in the Garden. They had enjoyed unbroken fellowship. How jarring it is to realize that, on this day, Adam is hiding from God! What a catastrophic change! Even reading about it from the long view of history, one is deeply dismayed at such a strange turn of events.

God's creature, made in God's own likeness, placed in a spectacularly lovely garden, given a plethora of tame animals and gorgeous and tasty plants to enjoy, given a wife to be a companion and helper to him, given meaningful and pleasant work to occupy his days, *given the very friendship of God Himself,* was hiding! Why?

I have to stop and think how lonely Adam must have been in hiding. Was Eve hiding with him? The following conversation with God was full of the pronoun, "I," so he certainly sounded alone. But even if Eve were with him, as it is clear that later she was, he had to have been very lonely. Truly, there is no loneliness like the empty feeling of having lost the fellowship of God after enjoying His unique presence and communication daily. For the very first time, Adam was estranged from God. That is powerful emptiness! Hiding is always accompanied by aching loneliness; hiding from God much more so.

God meant to alert Adam, and at least Adam answered God's question, and revealed the "why" of his actions rather honestly. "I heard the sound of you in the garden, and I was afraid." Fear is almost always the reason for hiding. Adam's hiding was both the most rational and irrational thing he could have done; rational because he was guilty of something awful, irrational because it could not succeed. No one can successfully hide from God. Adam was in a mess.

Hiding can be the actual, physical removal of one's body to a place of concealment, as in this case. More often it is hiding by disguise. Human beings hide by denying or distorting the truth, pretending to be something we are not, assuming a role we prefer to actually being our honest selves.

However hiding manifests itself, underneath is fear. We fear being exposed for who we truly are. We fear rejection. We fear being fully known by another, sure that being fully known would mean being unloved. The fear of being unloved is the deepest, scariest fear of all.

And so we hide, or try to hide, the parts of us that we consider unacceptable, because we crave acceptance and love. Sadly, even in what should be the most intimate relationships, human beings rarely allow themselves to be fully known. We all have secrets.

"Where are you?"

Adam admitted his fear. ". . . because I was naked. . ." With this confession, the jig was up. Adam could not have known about (and been ashamed of) his nakedness unless he had eaten of the fruit of the tree of the knowledge of good and evil, the only tree from which God had forbidden him to eat. Sin was exposed. Adam was unmasked, his secret revealed. Guilt lurks underneath fear.

Adam was yet to learn about grace. While we, along with Adam, are desperately hiding our guilty unacceptable selves least we be unloved, at the same time we long to be fully known *and* fully loved. We yearn to find someone who can love us completely, even while knowing everything (even the very worst) about us. To find *that* is truly paradise. Sadly, fearing we will never find it, we go on hiding.

Adam had yet to learn about grace. God, in all His divine perfections, is the One who knows everything about us: the best, the worst, and everything in between. Yet He loves us profoundly, mightily, lavishly. Words fail to describe the love of God. He is astoundingly in love with us. Adam was soon to be schooled in the amazing grace of God.

Before this conversation with Adam was finished, Eve and the serpent were included. It was to the serpent, the embodiment of Lucifer himself, the eternal enemy of God and His people—the devil, Satan—that God addressed the gospel that would change everything.

> I will put enmity between you and the woman,
> And between your offspring and her offspring;
> He shall bruise your head, and you shall bruise his heel.
> (Genesis 3:15)

Enemies are lined up here. All Lucifer's demons are sworn enemies of Adam and Eve and their children. Throughout the centuries of human history, there would be many occasions when the serpent—that is, the devil and his minions—would wound God's people. But heel wounds are not fatal. God's people would endure.

Eve's offspring ultimately was Jesus Christ, who would on the cross *fatally* wound the *head* of the serpent, the devil, Lucifer. Christ's death on the cross is the pivotal event of history because it totally defeated the serpent in his competition with God for supremacy in the lives of human beings.

This was the promise given to Adam and Eve as they stood in their ridiculous hiding place clothed in their pitiful garments of leaves.

Adam, did you hear that? Did you hear God's marvelous promise? Adam, do you get it? There is no need to hide. God knows all about you. There is nothing about you that He does not know. He knows what you did. Stop! He even knows what you thought, what you are thinking. And He loves you anyway. *He loves you!* He has a plan for your rescue. He is about to direct all future events to the fulfillment of His promise to redeem you and your offspring.

And just in case Adam and Eve didn't get it, God killed an animal and made fur skin clothing for them to wear. *The wages of sin is death, but the gift of God is eternal life through Jesus Christ our Lord.*

"*Where are you?*"

There is a poignant truth that initiates and permeates this narrative. *God pursued Adam!* Adam was not pursuing God. He was cringing in fear. Just as the Angel of the LORD pursued Hagar into the desert, so God had pursued Adam in the Garden of Eden. God was walking in the Garden calling Adam's name! This is the love of God on display at the outset of the human story.

I well remember a day when God called to me, "Where are you?" I did a poor job of hiding, because everyone around me saw the truth I was unwilling to admit. My method of hiding my anger was denial. I used many excuses to "justify" my temper. But the day came when I crossed a line even in my own estimation.

In extreme ire, I had wounded a friend so severely that he contemplated suicide. That was the occasion of my unmasking. It was my undoing. As soon as possible, I got to a quiet, alone place and confessed to my heavenly Father that I, like Adam, was naked and afraid.

That day I was able to face honestly the truth that I had deeply hurt a long list of people from my past and my present, and, though successful in many endeavors, I had failed in the very most important thing—loving.

And like Adam, that day I heard the gospel strong and clear. I experienced God's amazing love and grace that forgave me, and set me out on a journey of making amends to those I hurt—a journey not of shame, but of joy in restored relationships.

To all ashamed citizens of earth who long to be loved, but fear they cannot be loved *really*, God calls today, "Where are you?" Answer His tender, loving call. There is no need to hide. Knowing the worst about you, He died to forgive you. Even now He is lovingly preparing a place for you in heaven, because He doesn't want to be there for eternity without *you*.

"*Where are you?*"

For Further Thought

Psalm 139:1–12

Romans 5:1–21

Galatians 4:4

3

"Where is Abel your brother?"

GENESIS 4:9

Then the Lord said to Cain, "Where is Abel your brother?" He said, "I do not know; am I my brother's keeper?"

Two brothers, two vocations, two motivations, two offerings, two outcomes...

If anyone might be tempted to minimize the awful impact of the *fall* of Adam and Eve into sin, the story to follow from Genesis, chapter 4, must forever correct that misconception. The devastating result of sin entering the world of humans is tragically apparent in the first family.

Adam and Eve welcomed into the world their firstborn, a son whom they named Cain; and subsequently another son, whom they named Abel. This was the very first family.

Scripture is selective, rather than exhaustive, in its telling of history, having as its objective to reveal the unfolding of story of redemption through the ages. We are told in Scripture nothing about the childhoods of Cain and Abel. After the announcement of their births, we meet them next as adults, each having chosen a unique vocation. Cain became a farmer *(a worker of the ground)*, and Abel became a shepherd.

In time, Cain brought to the Lord an offering of the fruit of the ground. Likewise, Abel brought an offering consistent with his vocation—the firstborn sheep of his flock.

It seems all good, but there was a problem. God was pleased with Abel's offering, but He was not pleased with Cain's.

Some theologians have made the case that the difference in God's response to the two offerings had to do with the fact that Abel's offering involved the shedding of blood, an animal sacrifice—a symbolic act looking forward to the death of Jesus Christ for sinners. If this is the correct interpretation of God's positive response to Abel and negative response to Cain, it seems curious to me that nothing of the sort is mentioned as the events unfold in Genesis 4. We have there no information as to what Cain and Abel knew about future redemption. Indeed, it would be hundreds of years later, when Moses received the law of God, that the whole sacrificial system would be introduced, the system that would for sure symbolize the coming of Messiah, the Lamb of God, who would die for the sins of the world.

From the biblical narrative in Genesis 4, it appears clear that the crux of the matter is not the offerings themselves, but the hearts of the ones who presented their offerings. It is immediately apparent that Cain's heart was not right when he quickly became angry.

Cain was a competitor. Instead of offering his produce as an act of worship to God alone—the only thing that mattered—he compared God's response to him with God's response to Abel and became angry that his presentation was not as good as, or better than, Abel's.

The two offerings stemmed from two different motivations. Cain's was religious only, a dutiful act, while Abel's offering was an expression of his devotion to God, an act of worship. This is seen in God's further question to Cain, "If you do well, will you not be accepted?" It was not the offering; it was the man!

It is important to notice that God did not summarily reject Cain. In fact, God's mercy is clearly seen in His dealings with Cain. His first questions of Cain were actually, "Why are you angry, and why has your face fallen?" Ah, the competitor. . .Cain was angry because Abel achieved something that he, as the elder brother, had not—the favor of God.

Where is your brother?

This was Cain's opportunity to acknowledge his exposed heart. It was not too late to repent and be restored. God's love for Cain is seen in His warning to Cain: "If you do not do well, sin is crouching at the door. Its desire is for you, but you must rule over it." God was calling Cain to reject his performance of duty devoid of worship and devotion. He was calling Cain to turn away from his covetous attitude, his desire to be better than his younger brother. God was calling Cain to love Him alone.

But Cain paid no heed. He was consumed by his anger, and the unthinkable resulted. Cain murdered his brother. Could anyone have imagined this shocking occurrence? The first generation after Adam and Eve's creation, and the first family on earth is shattered by *fratricide*! THIS is the meaning of the *fall*. This is the awful result of Eve and Adam's agreement with the serpent. This is the potential for evil in every human heart not surrendered to God.

And this brings us to God's piercing question to Cain, *"Where is Abel your brother?"* After Cain killed his brother, was his anger spent? Perhaps. But his attitude was still rebellious.

Notice the difference between his answer to God's question, and Adam's answer to God's question. Adam was quick to own his predicament. He answered honestly, "I am hiding. . . I am afraid. . . I am naked." No such honesty from Cain. Instead, Cain first lies to God, claiming not to know where Abel is. Then, snarky, he answers the question with a sassy question of his own, challenging God, "Am I my brother's keeper?"

Cain shows himself to be unrepentant, belligerent, and God doesn't answer his pompous question. Instead, God pronounces judgment and punishment for Cain. But God makes provision to preserve Cain's life, even while seeing to it that his life will not be easy. The love and grace of God are unwavering, even for this miserable man.

Jesus answered the question that Cain posed to God. In Matthew 22: 37–40, Jesus' words are recorded: "You shall love the Lord your God with all your heart and with all your soul and with all your mind. This is the great and first commandment. And a second is like it: *You shall love your neighbor as yourself.* On these two commandments depend all the Law and the Prophets." In other words, the whole Old Testament required it.

> And this is the commandment we have from Him, whoever loves God must also love his brother.
> (1 John 4:21)

Throughout the New Testament, God broadens the term "brother" from actual, familial, blood brother to *fellow human being,* and especially to other members of the family of God. "And stretching out his hand toward his disciples, he said, 'Here are my mother and my brothers! For whoever does the will of my Father in heaven is my brother and sister and mother'" (Mark 3:35).

Where is your brother?

This story is instructive to us in at least three observations. First, it powerfully illustrates the importance of the instruction given in Proverbs 4:23: "Keep your heart with all vigilance. . . ." How ready we are to do good things for the wrong reasons! How easy it is for us to be religious instead of devoted to God who indicted Israel with the words, "You honor me with your lips, but your hearts are far from me" (see Isaiah 29:13). We offer things to God. We offer performances to God. What He wants is our hearts.

Secondly, when God nails us with a question, we must respond with honesty, gratitude, and repentance. God's questions are gracious, meant to rescue us. They are uncomfortable, but when answered with humility and faith, they bear really good fruit.

Most instructive of all, we *are* our brothers' keepers. Near the end of the Gospel of Matthew, Jesus pictures for us the future judgment. Hear His shocking words:

> When the Son of Man comes in His glory, and all the angels with Him, then He will sit on His glorious throne. Before Him will be gathered all the nations and He will separate people one from another as a shepherd separates the sheep from the goats. And He will place the sheep on His right, but the goats on the left. Then the King will say to those on His right, "Come you who are blessed by my Father, inherit the kingdom prepared for you from the foundation of the world. For I was hungry and you gave me food. I was thirsty and you gave me drink. I was a stranger and you welcomed me. I was naked and you clothed me. I was sick and you visited me. I was in prison and you came to me."
>
> Then the righteous will answer Him, saying, "Lord when did we see you hungry and feed you, or thirsty and give you drink? And when did we see you a stranger and welcome you or naked and clothe you? And when did we see you sick or in prison and visit you?" And the King will answer them, "Truly I say to you, as you did it to one of the least of these my *brothers*, you did it to me."
>
> Then He will say to those on His left, "Depart from me, you cursed, into the eternal fire prepared for the devil and his angels. For I was hungry and you gave me no food. I

"Where is Abel your brother?"

was thirsty and you gave me no drink. I was a stranger and you did not welcome me, naked, and you did not clothe me, sick and in prison and you did not visit me." Then they will answer, saying, "Lord, when did we see you hungry or thirsty or a stranger or naked or sick or in prison, and did not minister to you?" Then He will answer them, saying, "Truly I say to you, as you did not do it to one of the least of these [my brothers] you did not do it to me."
(Matthew 25:31–45)

Where is your brother?

I am a classic "Type A" personality. But for grace, I am ambitious. I am driven. I am a workaholic. I have enjoyed many successes throughout my life, but one day God nailed me with my *failure*. I had failed miserably in the only thing God cares about—loving. Loving Him first of all, and then loving my fellow human beings, my neighbor (in the words of Scripture).

My mother-in-law used to say, "We are to love people and use things, but we get it backward; we use people and love things." Boy, did that ever describe me. I wanted God to value and appreciate all my successes. I wanted to give them to God as offerings, but instead He broke my heart with my failure to love, and I had to go to Him with empty hands. In the words of the old hymn,

Foul, I to the fountain fly.
Wash me Savior, or I die.[2]

Where is your brother?

For Further Thought

Matthew 5:21–26

James 3:13–18

2 Augustus Toplady, *Rock of Ages*

4

"Who is this that darkens counsel by words without knowledge?"

JOB 38:2

"Who is this that darkens counsel by words without knowledge?"

Found near the end of the book of Job, this question cries out for examination, and the fruit of pondering it is enormously rewarding.

The books of the Bible are arranged purposefully, not exactly in chronological order. While the Bible is largely a book of history, it is a selective history, the main point being the story of redemption. After the books of Moses, we have the further historical books of Samuel, Kings, and Chronicles, followed by Ezra, Nehemiah, and Esther. Then before considering the prophets who spoke during the historical periods, we find a section of five books called the Wisdom Literature. They are Job, Psalms, Proverbs, Ecclesiastes, and the Song of Solomon. These books are more philosophical or perhaps more correctly, theological, in nature. However, they are not only intellectual in focus, as they contain some of the deepest heartfelt emotional content in Scripture. For example, Psalms is sometimes called accurately *the cry of the soul.* And the Song of Solomon is a romantic song for lovers.

The antiquity of the book of Job can be deduced by considering Job's long life and the absence of any mention in it of the law, the tabernacle, or the temple. Job probably lived in the patriarchal period, some scholars even suggesting that this book is the oldest book of the Bible. If so, the fact that Job is so enlightened theologically indicates that God provided a lot of revelation of Himself prior to Moses' writing of Scripture.

The book of Job is biographical. We don't know the author, but other Scriptures clearly treat Job as an historical figure. His story is, excepting the story of Jesus Christ, the most poignant of Scripture. His suffering is almost unthinkable.

We are told at the outset that Job was "blameless and upright, one who feared God and turned away from evil." Yet this good man, within a twenty-four-hour period, lost everything.

A very wealthy man in an agricultural economy, Job lost all his cattle, his buildings, most of his servants, and, most painful, all of his children. Finally, Job lost his health, so much so that he spent his days in the agony of physical pain. Piling on, his wife failed to support him, advising him to forget God and take his own life.

Anyone reading this story would be incredulous. Has there ever been another account of such extreme suffering? Almost any response from Job to his circumstances would be understandable.

But Job's initial response is not *understandable*. It is amazing—even for a man as devout as Job. Immediately upon hearing the news of the series of tragedies that befell him, he tore his robe and shaved his head. These customary signs of grief tell us that Job was human, and felt deeply the pain of his loss. But then he did something not customary, and profoundly meaningful. He "fell on the ground and worshiped." Really? Worshiped? His words of worship have been memorialized by Christians everywhere, throughout generations:

> Naked I came from my mother's womb, and naked shall I return. The LORD gave, and the LORD has taken away; blessed be the name of the LORD.
> (Job 1:21)

Wow! I wish I had this attitude when faced with much less adversity! I also wish that the book of Job ended with this doxology. But no, I really don't, because the remainder of the book is so instructive. Even godly Job had some things to learn!

Imperfect human beings, even very godly ones like Job, have mixed reactions to the painfulness of this broken world. Even Job could not maintain his worshipful perspective. We see throughout the next chapters the highs and lows of Job's emotions. At times he breaks through with wonderful statements of truth and faith. At other times he despairs, wishing he had never been born or longing for death.

Early on, Job was visited by three of his friends. They were great comforters at the beginning of their visit with Job. They just sat quietly with him. How I have wished for such friends. How

"Who is this that darkens counsel by words without knowledge?"

I have longed to be such a friend myself. People find it almost impossible to be quiet. In the face of suffering, we feel the need to *say something*. And that is where we, and Job's friends, go wrong. The bulk of the middle section of the book of Job is made up of the foolish talk of Job's friends, who masquerade as wise philosophers. They are so full of themselves. They are cold and condescending. They don't empathize with Job, and their arrogance prevents them from pointing him in the right direction.

It seems that Job goes wrong when he is goaded by his friends into defending himself against their accusations that he had somehow caused his own misfortune.

God is so patient. He allows the three friends to prattle on for a long time. Then He allows Job to defend himself. Job's argument sadly descends to the level of his friends' discourse.

Finally, after thirty some chapters of nonsense, God steps in. And His first words (out of the whirlwind) are a *question*!

"Who is this that darkens counsel by words without knowledge?"

And then God prepares Job for some rigorous testing. "Dress for action like a man; I will question you, and you make it known to me." I can hear a parent to a teenager, "You will answer me now, or I will know the reason why!" This is serious.

And then the questions come fast and furious. Here are some of them:

- "Where were you when I laid the foundation of the earth?"
- "Who determined the measurements—surely you know!"
- "Has the rain a father, or who has begotten the drops of dew?"
- "Can you bind the chains of the Pleiades, or loose the cords of Orion?"
- "Can you hunt the prey for the lion, or satisfy the appetite of the young lions?"
- "Do you know when the mountain goats give birth? Do you observe the calving of the does?"
- "Is it by your understanding that the hawk soars and spreads his wings toward the south?"

Then God gets to the heart of the matter: "Will you even put me in the wrong? Will you condemn me that you may be in the right?" (See Job 40:8.)

Job had been defending himself to his three friends. Knowing full well God's sovereign control over all things, Job's self-justification necessarily accused God of wrongdoing in allowing his painful experiences. It is the common reaction of people, even people of deep faith, to either implicitly or explicitly accuse God when hard trials come to them.

Dozens of questions later, Job is thoroughly humbled. I can imagine his body language as God questions him. He starts out head held high. Then he bows his head. Then his shoulders slump. Gradually his back bends over and he covers his face with his hands. There might even have been some tears sliding down his face.

Job's confession: ". . . I have uttered what I did not understand, things too wonderful for me, which I did not know. . . . I had heard of you by the hearing of the ear, but now my eye sees you, therefore I despise myself, and repent in dust and ashes."

This was a stunning reversal!

> . . . the LORD said to Eliphaz the Temanite: "My anger burns against you and against your two friends, for you have not spoken of me what is right as my servant Job has. Now therefore take seven bulls and seven rams and go to my servant Job and offer up a burnt offering for yourselves. And my servant Job shall pray for you, for I will accept his prayer not to deal with you according to your folly. For you have not spoken what is right as my servant Job has."
> (Job 42:7–8)

The three friends did as God commanded, and God accepted Job's prayer of their behalf.

The first stunning reversal is that instead of rebuking Job as He did for pages of Scripture, God referred to Job as "my servant" over and over again. This is grace. This is forgiveness. This is restoration.

The second stunning reversal is that God accepted Job's prayer

"Who is this that darkens counsel by words without knowledge?"

for his three friends. Before, the friends had arrogantly taken the position of Job's accusers. Now they are humbled as their accused friend intercedes with God for them. God's acceptance of Job as a supplicant shows that Job is reinstated as a devout and holy man.

The third stunning reversal (and it is no doubt third in importance, but none the less significant) is God's restoring to Job all he had lost and more! The Lord gave to Job twice as much as he had before!

I remember in the fresh acid pain of recent divorce, how I questioned God. Naively, I had assumed that because I was a born-again Christian and was doing my best to follow the Lord and serve Him, that nothing bad would ever happen to me—at least nothing *really bad*. Now I accused God of not keeping His promises to me. One day I was standing in my dining room, the hub of our house, and I thought, "Maybe God isn't real at all. Maybe I have just believed some myth my parents taught me. Maybe I should just abandon Christianity with all its rules and standards, and just live my life for all the satisfaction I can get (after all, I was forty-nine, and remaining life seemed short). Well, that thinking lasted only a few seconds! There came immediately over me a strong assurance that God is exactly who He revealed Himself to be in Scripture, my experience notwithstanding. I went and picked out from our bookcase my childhood hymnal and sat down at the piano. Tears streaming down my face, I played and sang some of those old hymns, and discovered that the old hymn writers must have suffered because there was a lot about suffering in the words of those old hymns, and great encouragement.

Much later, two truths changed everything and set me on the road to recovery from grief.

First truth: My life is not a mistake. It is part of God's plan. In ways I cannot understand, my life fits into God's overall plan of redemption.

Second truth: God does not exist to make me happy. Rather, I was created for His glory. I live for Him, not the other way around. So, the only proper outcome is that I live out my life for His glory.

"Who is this that darkens counsel by words without knowledge?"

❖

For Further Thought

Isaiah 55:6–11
Daniel 4:28–37 (especially verses 34–37)
Romans 11:33–36

❖

"Who is this that darkens counsel by words without knowledge?"

5

"What is your name?"

GENESIS 32:27

And he said to him, "What is your name?" And he said, "Jacob."

What is more significant to your being than your name? Your name is your identity. For good or ill, for fame or infamy, you are known by your name. This was even more significant in Bible days when names were more closely linked to family, to a particular location, or sometimes to a vocation or trade.

> Fear not, for I have redeemed you; I have *called you by name,* you are mine.
> (Isaiah 43:1)

> ... rejoice that your *names* are written in heaven.
> (Luke 10:20)

God thinks of each of us individually *by name.* And God relates to Jacob *by name.*

Oh, Jacob! His life's story rivals the best-selling thrillers of our day. It bests some of the blockbuster motion picture sagas ever seen.

Jacob was destined to play a major role in God's unfolding of redemption's story. But Jacob would not be ready for God's purposes for him for some time. Jacob had to go through an extensive preparation. *Because*...Jacob was headstrong. Jacob was willful. Jacob was ambitious and greedy and driven to dominate.

He would never be content to be the *younger* brother.

God surely created Jacob to be a strong leader, but his leadership qualities had to be refined. To use other metaphors, Jacob was a rough-hewn log that would need a lot of whittling, a lump of clay that would need the skill of the master potter, a bucking bronco that would need to be broken.

His name actually means "He takes by the hand," or "He cheats." Was his naming a prophetic vision of his future? Esau was born first, and when Jacob was born, he came out with his hand holding Esau's heel—a clear sign of aggression. In my imagination, I can almost see the fetus Jacob grabbing Esau's heel, crying without words, "But you can't be first!" (as if he could stop Esau's birth and pass him in the womb). I can also imagine the boyhoods of twins Jacob and Esau. I can picture them competing as Cain and Abel surely did.

The boys were very different. Esau grew up to be a skillful hunter, an outdoorsman. He loved the fields, the woods, the streams. He must have been rough in his appearance, sun- and wind-burned and muscled. We know from Scripture that he was hairy—thus his name.

Jacob, on the other hand, was quiet, preferring the indoor life of domestic activity. Even his physical appearance contrasted with Esau's. Jacob was smooth skinned. Keeping to the house, he was probably pale and more delicate. Another big difference between them was that Isaac, the father, loved Esau; but Rebekah loved Jacob, *a portent of things to come.*

Esau was not ambitious and driven as was Jacob. He was weak willed, laid back, easy going; and Jacob took advantage of Esau's easy-to-be-manipulated character.

First, knowing that Esau would be very hungry when he came in from the fields and woods at the end of the day, Jacob made a delicious stew and then bribed Esau into giving up his birthright for a mere bowl of it! The birthright was a big deal. It set apart the eldest son as the leader of the family, the inheritor of the father's legacy. It was a big deal legally, socially, and, most important, spiritually. Somehow Esau didn't catch the significance of it. He was hungry, after all. The bowl of stew was irresistible. Esau was too easy to influence. And Jacob obtained the birthright he had been coveting.

The second "cheat" was a bit more dramatic, and Jacob had an accomplice—his mother, Rebekah. She wanted Jacob to have the place of prominence that Esau acquired when he was born first. Father Isaac was very old and nearly blind. His death was imminent. It was time to give the formal, ceremonial blessing to the firstborn of the family, who would carry on the father's legacy. With his mother's help, Jacob had to disguise himself by draping animal skins on his body to cover his relatively hairless skin, by wearing his brother's outdoor-smelling clothes, and by preparing game for Isaac as Esau was accustomed to doing. The subterfuge worked, and Isaac gave Jacob the firstborn's blessing.

As expected, Esau was furious when he learned that his blessing had been stolen by Jacob. (Evidently, he valued the blessing more than he valued the birthright.)

Esau's fury was such that Jacob was forced to flee for his life. He packed a few belongings and some provisions, and left on a journey to his mother's home and her father, Bethuel, in Haran, where he hoped to find a wife from among the daughters of Laban, Rebekah's brother.

"What is your name?"

In Laban, Jacob met his match! Laban was no less deceitful, crafty, and manipulative than Jacob. The cheater would be cheated time and again. Yet God's love and care for Jacob is clear. Jacob prospered in spite of Laban's treachery, outwitting him time after time, and becoming a very rich man.

Laban realized he had been outfoxed by Jacob more than a few times, and was unhappy about it. Tensions brewed between Laban and Jacob.

Behind the scenes in Haran, God was working all things out for the accomplishment of His redemptive plan, and Jacob's role in it. One night, the angel of God came to Jacob in a dream and said to him, "I have seen all that Laban is doing to you. I am the God of Bethel. . . . Now arise, go out from this land and return to the land of your kindred."

It was time to leave Laban, and leaving Laban meant finally, dangerously, after many years, confronting his brother Esau.

Was Esau still murderously angry? Were Jacob's vast possessions in peril, not to mention his large family, including many children? Including his own life?

A poignant scene ensues: Jacob sends his wives, his children and all the he has ahead of him across the ford, or stream, called Jabbok.

Jacob had sent messengers ahead to Esau's camp to prepare

Esau for Jacob's arrival. They returned with the information that Esau had four hundred men with him. (All Jacob had was wives, children, servants, and livestock.)

Genesis 32:7 states, "Then Jacob was greatly afraid and distressed." In verse 11, we have his prayer recorded, "Please deliver me from the hand of my brother, for I fear him. . ." Smart, shrewd, cunning, crafty, cheating Jacob *was afraid*. Perhaps for the first time in his life, he was out of his depth. Jacob's courage failed him. What would tomorrow bring?

That night, with his precious family on the other side of the stream, Jacob couldn't sleep. "And a man wrestled with him until the breaking of the day" (Genesis 32:24). When the man saw that he was not prevailing against Jacob, he dealt the final blow. He touched Jacob's hip socket and put Jacob's hip out of joint. At the same time, he asked to be excused, for the day had broken.

But Jacob famously said, "I will not let you go unless you bless me." Jacob knew it was God. He later named the place *Peniel*, declaring that he had seen God face-to-face, *Peniel* meaning *the face of God*.

Jacob prevailed in the open-air arena of physical combat, but God won the day. God triumphed. God *has* to win. God has to rule. God is Sovereign of the cosmos. "For Yours is the kingdom and the power and the glory forever and ever" (Matthew 6:13, NKJV). He controls all things. God has to be and *is* Commander-in-chief. How do I know that God won? Because Jacob would not be satisfied without God's blessing. Jacob prevailed on the wrestling field, but God prevailed in the far more important turf of Jacob's heart! God's purpose was not to make Jacob weak and ineffectual. It was to show him who is boss.

Think of it! Jacob had arrived in Haran with nothing, and was leaving a very wealthy, enormously successful man. He had accomplished a great deal. He had a huge family. He was smart, strategically smart. *But this man knew he needed God's blessing.* He no longer wanted to live by his wits. He wanted to live by God's power at work within him. His heart was changed.

His limped for the rest of his life. I want to think of this as a lovely, gracious limp. With every step he took, he was reminded that God had won his heart. He was reminded that God was in control. God is Sovereign.

In response to Jacob's determination to get God's blessing, God asked the curious question,

"What is your name?"

Surely God knew Jacob's name. But He wanted Jacob to own it. He wanted Jacob to own his history, the whole narrative of who he was and what he had done—his accomplishments and his crooked ways of achieving them—the whole wretched business.

And then, breathtakingly, God recognizes something very good in Jacob, and changes his name to reflect it, and to signify that he indeed is a changed man.

God changed Jacob's name to *Israel,* which means *he strives with God.* God is no insignificant opponent. And yet, all night Jacob fought Him and prevailed physically. The fact that God commended Jacob for this by changing his name to memorialize it gives me great encouragement.

Yes, Jacob needed to be conquered, but the fact that he didn't fold at the first struggle shows good character in Jacob. If God was going to fight with him, then Jacob was going to hang on to God to the bitter end.

Life in this broken world just teems with mysteries, questions, and complexities. Daily we face things we do not understand. Why are precious innocent children abused? Why are faithful saints confined to sick beds? Why do young people die before their time? Why are our leaders allowed to be corrupt? Why heartbreak and betrayal?

Thinking people of faith cry out to God for answers. The *whys* are not necessarily rebellious, disrespectful accusations, but heartfelt longings to know God in the midst of life that so often does not make sense.

God's renaming of Jacob tells me that God honors our sincere questions, even as He knows that this side of heaven our insufficient intellects will not be satisfied. We can never understand the Almighty, but it is a noble effort to try to do so. God never chides us for our honest confusion and doubt. Faith wrestles with God again and again; and, like Jacob, learns that God is King. With Job and with Jacob, wounded saints learn to listen and to trust. Finally, the wrestling comes to an end, and faith is quiet. *Be still and know that I am God.*

A Christian missionary who served God for decades in a place of extreme poverty and other forms of human degradation was heard to say (tongue in cheek), "When I get to heaven, God is going to have a lot of explaining to do!" She wrestled with God on behalf of people she had come to love.

I have wrestled with God through painful betrayal and divorce, through emotional and verbal abuse, through the suffering of my children, through the lostness of grandchildren, through sharp loneliness, and through the sadness of dear friends.

I think I have asked God all the hardest questions. I have received only partial answers—for *now we see through a glass darkly*. I am so glad God allows our honest, sincere *whys*. I am so glad that God bears our childish misunderstandings.

"What is your name?"

I want to be known as a striver with God. I don't want to paint over the difficult thoughts. To do so is to live superficially. I want to live authentically. If a battle is to be fought, let us fight it for real.

"What is your name?"

❖

"What is your name?"

For Further Thought

Philippians 2:9–11

Hebrews 11:32–39

❖

6

"What is that in your hand?"

EXODUS 4:2

The Lord said to him, "What is that in your hand?" He said, "A staff."

Moses' extraordinary beginning was surely the harbinger of an extraordinary life. Born a slave, Moses was not supposed to live at all. His survival, initially, was due to the faith of a God-fearing Hebrew midwife who defied Pharaoh, the ruler of Egypt who wanted all male Hebrew slave babies to be killed at birth. Moses also somehow escaped drowning in the Nile River, which was to be the fate of all those who made it through the birth process. Ironically, Pharaoh tried, but failed, to kill his future adoptive grandson!

Hebrews 11:23 continues the story with beautiful brevity: "By faith Moses, when he was born, was hidden for three months by his parents, because they saw that the child was beautiful, and they were not afraid of the king's edict." When one fears God, one does not fear lesser beings.

With uncommon courage born of deep trust in God, his dear mother, when she could hide the child no longer, made a basket from stout grasses, waterproofed it with tar, placed her beautiful child in it, and floated it in the Nile River. Placed in tall river grasses close to shore, the basket was carefully watched by big sister.

The little boat was found by Pharaoh's daughter, who, though she recognized him as a Hebrew slave child, had compassion on Moses. Big sister was quick to suggest that she find a Hebrew nursemaid for him, to which Pharaoh's daughter agreed. Of course, the nursemaid was Moses' own birth mother!

A mother myself, I can (but at the same time, cannot) imagine those early years of Moses. Knowing that at some point, probably sooner rather than later, she would have to give him back to Pharaoh's daughter, his mother must have treasured those precious years. Moses' future choices make it clear that Jochebed did more than care for his young body. She undoubtedly nurtured his soul. She wisely taught him the faith; that is, the truth of the God of Abraham, Isaac, and Jacob.

When Moses was weaned, Jochebed returned him to Pharaoh's daughter who began to raise him as her own son. How hard it must have been to give him up! She must have prayed for him every day of her life.

Meanwhile Moses had dual citizenship. Surely the culture of Egypt, not to mention the culture of the palace, was far different from the customs of the Hebrews. But Moses was not confused. His actions as an adult show that he identified with his Hebrew heritage, and felt the sting of the slavery of his people.

He could not tolerate seeing a fellow Hebrew being beaten by an Egyptian, and, vigilante-like, killed the Egyptian. The next day, he realized that his lawless action was known, even by Pharaoh, who wanted to kill him. And so Moses fled from all he had known, both in Goshen with his Hebrew family, and in the palace at Memphis with his Egyptian family. He went to the desert land of Midian.

Some scholars have divided Moses' life into three roughly equal parts—forty years in Egypt as Pharaoh's grandson, forty years as a shepherd in the desert of Midian, and forty years as the leader of the exodus of the Hebrews from Egypt and their journey to Canaan, the land of promise.

I must pause here to reflect on God's timetable compared to mine. Moses was approximately eighty years old when he became the leader of God's people. Those first eighty years of his life were not uneventful, or wasted. The child of slaves, a rich and privileged young prince, a lowly shepherd—in God's providence, no experience is wasted. Moses was in God's school. He was being shaped by loving discipline into the person God would call to the very important task of leading the exodus. God is not in a hurry. He is infinitely patient. He knows what He is doing; and, unlike us, He dwells in eternity.

I am not patient. I've got places to go, people to meet, things to do! I am in a hurry. I want results. I want to see progress—now—in myself and in the people I care about.

"Be still and know that I am God" (Psalm 46:10) *Be still* can mean "Be quiet," but it can also mean "Cease activity." When I find that difficult, I am comforted to know that God is in charge and that He ignores my timetable and does His gracious work.

So we come to God's question of Moses. His forty years in the desert of Midian are about to come to an end because God is ready to make His move. He has heard the cries of His people. It is time to rescue them from slavery, and Moses, oblivious to what is coming, is His chosen leader.

Moses, now married, is shepherding his father-in-law, Jethro's, flock near Horeb. There he encounters a very strange sight indeed. A bush is burning fiercely, but is not consumed. It just continues to burn with the same intensity, but with no apparent effect on the bush! Curious, Moses turns aside to investigate, when he hears the voice of God calling to Him from the middle of the bush. "Moses, Moses." When Moses signals his awareness, God warns him not to come closer, but to remove his shoes, as the ground itself is holy, so near is it to the presence of the Most High God.

And then God tells Moses in some detail His plans for removing the Hebrews from their enslavement in Egypt, and His destination for them. The picture is one of great victory. They won't simply sneak out of Egypt cowed and shamed. No, they will plunder Egypt, much of the wealth of Egypt coming into their possession. Embedded in the presentation is God's intention to send Moses to Pharaoh to secure the release of the slaves (who, after all, built the empire).

Since *Pharaoh* is a title and not a name, we do not know with any certainty if the Pharaoh who reigned during the exodus was the same Pharaoh who reigned when Moses was born. Could it be the same Pharaoh, Moses' angry, vengeful grandfather—the same one who threated his life the last time he was in Egypt? It was a long time ago, but still. . .

And the Hebrews—they had grown used to slavery. Yes, life was hard, but if they angered Pharaoh, it could get a lot harder. Yes, they did punishing work, kept punishing hours, but they ate well, didn't they? Leave Egypt?. . . Risk so much? . . . It would be a hard sell.

Moses protested to God. He listed a series of reasons why he was not the man for the job. The first was that he would not be believed, or even listened to. No one would perceive that God Himself had sent him. God's response to Moses' remonstrating was a question.

"What is that in your hand?"

Answer: *A staff.* Of course, this was Moses' standard equipment. He was a shepherd. He was tending sheep that very day. *A staff!* A simple shepherd's crook—the most common, unpretentious item ever. Like a pencil to an accountant, like a wooden spoon to a cook, like a hammer to a carpenter, or a shovel to a gardener, it was a cheap, common tool, surely made from a tree branch. It was nothing, really. It was unlikely to be remarked upon.

But in God's work, the simplest, most ordinary thing becomes a useful tool for an eternal purpose.

"Moses, throw it on the ground." When he did so, the staff became a snake, so scary that Moses ran from it. When, at God's direction, he grabbed it by the tail, it became his staff again. This demonstration was to convince the people that God had sent Moses—for real.

"What is that in your hand?"

Moses had a shepherd's staff in his hand. So did David, who was also a shepherd. But David also had a slingshot in his hand. With it he had protected his flock and killed predators that would have killed some sheep for food.

With that same common slingshot, David killed the giant Goliath, who, along with his army of Philistines, threatened the people of God.

David also frequently had something else in his hand. He had a harp. It was a simple, handmade instrument with which he passed the time in the pasture with his sheep. He became a skilled musician, and later wrote most of Israel's hymnbook, called *The Psalms*. The music has been lost to us, but the beautiful words expressing the cry of the soul, both in anguish and in praise, assures us that the music must also have been wonderful.

"What is that in your hand?"

I am thinking of the widow of Zarephath. Elijah, the prophet of God, had announced God's intention to chasten His rebellious people by way of a famine. The famine was severe, but God had promised to take care of His servant. Of all things, God instructed Elijah to go to a particular widow who would feed him.

When Elijah approached her, she had in her hand a bundle of sticks with which to start a fire, over which she would bake a couple small loaves of unleavened bread.

More significantly, she had in her hand a small quantity of flour and very little oil. She was sure that the small loaves would be barely enough for her and her son to have one last meal. Death was stalking her.

I gasp when I think of what Elijah's request for food must have meant to her. It must have been unthinkable to withhold food from her son! What great faith she had! Either she trusted God to provide for her and her son as she gave her last provision to Elijah, or she did not fear death. God did indeed provide for her.

A few sticks, a handful of flour, and few tablespoons of oil—so little, so ordinary, but in God's providence, so *much*.

"What is that in your hand?"

I am thinking of an incident in the life of Jesus, also involving food. Jesus had been preaching all day. The people were rapt in attention, blown away by His words of eternal life. The day was waning. It was past dinnertime. The disciples suggested that it was time to dismiss the people. But Jesus had compassion on them. Knowing that they had not eaten all day, knowing they would return home on foot, He didn't want them to faint on the way home from lack of nourishment. He instructed the disciples to feed them. Feed them? With what? There were over 10,000 people if you count women and children.

A lad had a lunch, not much really—just five small cakes of unleavened bread, and two small fish. It was a boy's lunch, no more. But when given to Jesus, it miraculously fed all the people. Leftovers demonstrated that everyone was satisfied.

"What is that in your hand?"

In my hand was a piano. Well, so to speak, since a piano is the least portable of all musical instruments, excepting the pipe organ. After the pain of my divorce subsided somewhat, I wanted very much to fulfill a lifelong desire to be a missionary. Having many family friends in India, I was attracted to a small Bible college there. But what would I do there? How would I fit in?

I am far from a great musician, but I am a competent piano player, and I had been a piano teacher most of my adult life. The Bible college was lacking in the area of music. The piano is not portable. No matter. I sold my piano in the States, and bought a piano in India.

I happily became the worship leader and piano teacher to a beautiful and precious group of gifted, but previously untrained, Indian students.

In God's providence, what is ordinary and unremarkable becomes a significant tool for His redemptive purposes.

In the church where, growing up, I worshiped with my family, there was a fellow church member in whose hand were scissors, a comb, and a razor. He was a barber. On his days off, he would go into the local hospitals and nursing homes and offer free haircuts and shaves to any men who wanted them. While he groomed them, he talked to them about Jesus.

"What is that in your hand?"

❖

"What is that in your hand?"

For Further Thought

1 Samuel 17:12–49 (especially verse 40)
Nehemiah 4:15–23
Matthew 27:57–61
Luke 21:1–4

❖

7

"Whom shall I send, and who will go for us?"

ISAIAH 6:8

And I heard the voice of the Lord saying, "Whom shall I send, and who will go for us?" Then I said, "Here I am! Send me."

The book of Isaiah stands tall among the sacred, inspired writings of Scripture. It is the largest of all the prophetic books; indeed, the largest and most expansive book of the Bible. Its size, however, is secondary to its breadth of revelation. Its sweep of history is formidable, from the counsels of God in eternity past to the final redemption of all creation.

Its descriptions of God, from His glorious transcendence ("It is He who sits above the circle of the earth, and its inhabitants are like grasshoppers; who stretches out the heavens like a curtain, and spreads them like a tent to dwell in; who brings princes to nothing and makes the rulers of the earth as emptiness."—Isaiah 40:22, 23) to His sweet and gentle immanence ("He will tend his flock like a shepherd; he will gather the lambs in his arms; he will carry them in his bosom, and gently lead those that are with young."—Isaiah 40:11) and ("Fear not, for I have redeemed you; I have called you by name, you are mine. . . you are precious in my eyes, and honored, and I love you. . ."—Isaiah 43:1, 4) take one's breath away.

The designation *prophet* simply means *preacher*. Isaiah, the preacher, was the son of Amoz. He preached in Judah over a span of sixty years, during which Israel was carried away captive, and Judah was invaded. The shadow of the mighty Assyrian empire was the backdrop of Isaiah's revelation. Isaiah preached to (and during the reigns of) four kings: Uzziah, Jotham, Ahaz, and Hezekiah.

The book of Isaiah contains beautiful words of comfort. How many broken saints have been revived by the sweet balm of these words ". . .they who wait for the LORD shall renew their strength; they shall mount up with wings like eagles; they shall run and not be weary; they shall walk and not faint" (Isaiah 40:31). Or "When you pass through the waters, I will be with you;

and through the rivers, they shall not overwhelm you; when you walk through fire you shall not be burned, and the flame shall not consume you. For I am the LORD, your God, the Holy One of Israel, your Savior" (Isaiah 43:2, 3). Or "Come, everyone who thirsts, come to the waters; and he who has no money, come, buy and eat! Come, buy wine and milk, without money and without price" (Isaiah 55:1).

Isaiah employs sharp and colorful language to make his messages clear. Imagine hearing this: "From the sole of the foot even to the head, there is no soundness in it, but bruises and sores and raw wounds; they are not pressed out or bound up or softened with oil" (Isaiah 1:6). Or, "Instead of perfume there will be rottenness; and instead of a belt, a rope; and instead of well-set hair, baldness; and instead of a rich robe, a skirt of sackcloth; and branding instead of beauty" (Isaiah 3:24).

In the book of Isaiah, we find some of the most beautiful and most clear predictions concerning the coming Messiah. Christ's birth is foretold in 7:14 and 9:6, His deity in 9:6, 7, His ministry in 9:1, 2; 42:1–7 and 61:1,2, His death in 52:1–53:12, and His future reign in chapters 2, 11, 65 and more.

After a powerful introduction to God's indictment of Israel and Judah, come His forecast of judgment, and His offer of grace, atonement, and healing; in chapter 6, Isaiah relates his experience of calling—one might even say "anointing"—to be God's messenger.

Not to be preachy, but I cannot help but see four clear parts to Isaiah's call, and it serves as a kind of template for God's call to every human being. The four parts are: God's revelation of Himself in Isaiah's vision; Isaiah's confession of uncleanness as a direct result of seeing the vision; the atonement of Isaiah's sin and his forgiveness; and finally, Isaiah's commission.

It is the template for God's everlasting work in the soul of every man. First, He reveals Himself. Through that perspective, He leads the person to repentance. Upon one's confession of guilt, He forgives one's sin on the basis of Christ's atonement on the cross. When a person is forgiven and cleansed, he is then given the work he is to do. It has happened countless times throughout human history. It happened to me.

"Whom shall I send, and who will go for us?"

Chapter six begins: "In the year that King Uzziah died, I saw the LORD sitting upon a throne, high and lifted up; and the train of his robe filled the temple." Isaiah also saw angelic beings, called *seraphim*, who called antiphonally about the holiness and glory of God. He is called the "LORD of the heavenly armies" by them.

Holiness denotes *otherness*, that God is unique among everything and everyone in existence past, present, and future. There is no one like Him. Surely this vision of holiness, glory, seraphim, robe, and train capture that idea quite well!

Glory denotes dazzling beauty and surpassing goodness.

Confirming the transcendent quality of the vision, an earthquake ensued, and smoke filled the house where Isaiah was.

Seeing God is a remarkable gift. It clarifies everything. All else is brought into perspective. And so Isaiah's response was completely logical. He saw himself as he truly was in the presence of God's holiness and glory. His confession: "Woe is me! For I am lost; for I am a man of unclean lips; and I dwell in the midst of a people of unclean lips; for my eyes have seen the King, the LORD of hosts!" Clearly, Isaiah saw himself as a sinner, and he admitted it openly.

Why did he focus his confession on "lips"? Lips here is a metaphor for the heart, the unclean heart. In Matthew 12:34, Jesus said, "For out of the abundance of the heart the mouth speaks." Lips always convey the condition of the heart. "Lips" also stand for "words." Did Isaiah somehow realize at this point that God was calling him to preach—to use his *lips* to speak words of eternal life?

After Isaiah's admitting his uncleanness and implied cry for help—"Woe is me!"—a curious thing happened. One of the seraphim took from the altar a burning coal, flew to Isaiah, and touched his mouth with the coal. This action was an object lesson, heat being a method of cleansing or sterilization. Indeed, the seraphim then announced the most beautiful words a sinner could ever hear: "Your guilt is taken away, and your sin atoned for." Atonement implies the payment of a price to remove guilt. Thus, the third part of the call.

Isaiah's confession, followed by his forgiveness, led to the question which is the focal point of this chapter, a question posed to him by the voice of the Lord.

"Whom shall I send, and who will go for us?"

I have puzzled over why the Lord used a question to commission Isaiah to preach. Why not just command him to go, as God did with the other prophets?

Most of those prophets—Moses, Jeremiah, Elijah, to name a few—protested. One, namely Jonah, rebelled outright and went the other way.

In this case, God threw out a kind of general question. Based on God's remarkable revelation of Himself to Isaiah, and His powerful atonement of Isaiah, He gave Isaiah the opportunity to give Himself in service to the only One who is worthy. "Who will go. . . ?" I am reminded of an old hymn called *When I Survey the Wondrous Cross*. The last verse reads:

> *Were the whole realm of nature mine,*
> *that were a present far too small;*
> *love so amazing, so divine*
> *demands my soul, my life, my all.*[3]

"Whom shall I send, and who will go for us?"

It is a two-part question, each part having a different subject. "Whom shall I send. . ."—God's activity (sending). "*Who* will go for us?"—the preacher's activity (going). Going is predicated on God's sending. The preacher will have to face criticism and rejection, but one can face anything knowing that the only sovereign God, Lord of Creation, Ruler of the nations, God of wisdom, love, and power has sent him.

God needed a preacher. There is a pattern throughout Scripture, a pattern that all good teachers should try to follow. First, God always tells His people what He is going to do. He announces His intentions, in many cases serving as a warning. Then He does what He said He would do. Then He explains what He did—prophecy, history, doctrine.

Take, for example, the life and ministry of Jesus Christ. We have in the Old Testament Scriptures many prophecies of the coming of

---

[3] Isaac Watts, *When I Survey the Wondrous Cross*

"Whom shall I send, and who will go for us?"

the Messiah. In the Gospels we have the actual historical account of His birth, life, death, ascension, and promise of return. In the epistles we have the explanation of His life and redeeming work. In the epistles we find the reasons for His incarnation, His perfect life, His atoning death, His ascension to the Father's right hand, and His return to complete His work by literally redeeming all of creation, including our bodies.

Old Testament Israel had wandered far from God. Their lawlessness was so pervasive that even their religious observances were an abomination to God.

> Hear the word of the LORD. . .I have had enough of burnt offerings of rams. . .I do not delight in the blood of bulls. . .bring no more vain offerings; incense is an abomination to me. . .your new moons and your appointed feasts my soul hates; they have become a burden to me. (Isaiah 1:10–14)

Whom the Lord loves, He chastens (see Hebrews 12:6). God had to chasten His wayward people. He was planning to use the Assyrian empire and then the Babylonian empire to crush His people. But first, He must announce what He is going to do. The purpose of prophecy is never simply to satisfy curiosity about future events. The purpose is twofold. It is, first of all, to give incentive and time for people to repent. And second, to give encouragement to the "remnant" of the nation who had not turned away from God, because prophecies of judgment always include promises of future restoration. They also include warm assurances of God's presence and love during the worst of times.

Perhaps the best example of the latter purpose is found in the book of Lamentations, which is a companion to the book of Jeremiah. It is an expression of terrible grief over God's judgment of the nation. But right in the middle of the suffering we find a beautiful balm to the soul:

> Remember my affliction and my wanderings, the wormwood and the gall! My soul continually remembers it and is bowed down within me. But this I call to mind and

therefore I have hope: The steadfast love of the LORD never ceases; His mercies never come to an end; they are new every morning; great is your faithfulnes.
(Lamentations 3:19-23)

To announce His purposes for the future, God needed a preacher. After revealing Himself to Isaiah, leading him to repentance, forgiving and cleansing him, God presents His need of a preacher to Isaiah.

Whom shall I send, and who will go for us [the Holy Trinity]?

Isaiah's response was immediate. *"Here I am! Send me."* The exclamation point seems to me to convey the idea that Isaiah was eager. "Here" means "present now." I picture a child in the classroom waving his hand in the air, so eager for the teacher to call on him! "Here! Me!" Isaiah was not a reluctant conscript. He really longed to serve God.

I am thinking of another old hymn, written by Frances Ridley Havergal:

Take my life and let it be consecrated, Lord, to Thee. . .take my moments and my days. . .take my hands. . .take my feet. . .take my voice. . .take my intellect. . .take my silver and my gold, not a mite would I withhold. . .take my love, take my heart. . .take myself and I will be, ever only all for Thee.[4]

This is the cry of a broken sinner who has been rescued, redeemed, forgiven, cleansed, restored.

I am that broken sinner. I owed a debt I could never possibly pay. Jesus paid that debt for me. The words of Isaiah, of Ms. Havergal, and *When I Survey the Wondrous Cross* are my words.

"Whom shall I send, and who will go for us?"

❖

[4] Frances Ridley Havergal, *Take My Life*

"Whom shall I send, and who will go for us?"

For Further Thought

Romans 10:14–17
Romans 12:1,2
2 Corinthians 5:14,15
James 3

❖

8

"Have I not commanded you?"

JOSHUA 1:9

Have I not commanded you? Be strong and courageous. Do not be frightened, and do not be dismayed, for the Lord your God is with you wherever you go."

"Have I not commanded you? Be strong and courageous. Do not be frightened, and do not be dismayed, for the LORD your God is with you wherever you go" (Joshua 1:9).

The question is asked of Joshua, son of Nun, an Ephraimite. Nun is known in the Bible exclusively as the father of Joshua. Joshua, like Joseph, and unlike some other significant characters in Scripture (Noah, Samson, David, Solomon) had no apparent moral lapses during his life. It appears from Scripture that Joshua was faithful to God from his youth, and continuing throughout his life.

Why the command, and why the question preceding it?

The background to this command is God's call for Joshua to succeed Moses as the leader of the nation of Israel—namely, to lead them into Canaan, the land God promised Israel when they left Egypt.

Joshua had been Moses' assistant from his youth. He had been at Moses' side at crucial times in the nation's history through the forty-year trek through the desert. For example, he was with Moses on Mount Sinai, the mountain of God, when Moses received the Ten Commandments (Exodus 24:13; 32:17). Moses set up a tent outside the camp of the people where he would meet God and God would talk to him face-to-face. It was there that anyone could go to seek the Lord. When Moses entered the tent, the pillar of cloud would descend and stand at the entrance of the tent, and, seeing it, the people would worship. When Moses left the tent, his young assistant, Joshua, would not depart from it.

As Moses' companion and helper, Joshua had a unique position from which to learn the ways of God and to come to know God personally. His devotion is noteworthy.

Now, Joshua is at the most significant crossroads of his life. Moses is dead. Moses had disobeyed God, and as a consequence was not to continue as the leader of the people, particularly as they crossed the Jordan River into the land God had promised to give them. Before he died, Moses had named Joshua as his successor, and now God confirmed that call in His own words to Joshua: ". . . the LORD said to Joshua, the son of Nun, Moses' assistant, 'Moses my servant is dead. Now therefore arise, go over this Jordan, you and all this people, into the land that I am giving to them, to the people of Israel'" (Joshua 1:1,2).

The subsequent command could be stated, "Have I not commanded you to be strong and courageous. . .?"

It is interesting that Joshua previously gave the same instruction to the nation. Joshua was among the twelve spies, representing the twelve tribes of Israel, to embark on a reconnaissance of the land of Canaan, which God promised to give them. Of the twelve, only Joshua and Caleb came back with a positive report. Joshua said to the people, ". . . do not fear the people of the land. . .their protection is removed from them, and the LORD is with us; *do not fear them*" (Numbers 14:9).

Now Joshua hears the same command from the Lord. "Be strong and courageous. Do not be frightened and do not be dismayed. . . ."

To be strong is to be tough, tenacious, hardy, effectual. In the context it denotes strength of character—strong of will, able to stand firm, able to resist. I am reminded of Paul's words to the Corinthian church at the end of his famous chapter on the resurrection. After the stunning words, "Death is swallowed up in victory. O death, where is your victory? O death, where is your sting? Thanks be to God, who gives us the victory through our Lord Jesus Christ," he writes, "Therefore, my beloved brothers be steadfast, immovable, always abounding in the work of the Lord, knowing that in the Lord your labor is not in vain." (See 1 Corinthians 15:54-58.) That is the definition of strength!

To be courageous is to be brave, bold, intrepid, valiant. It is the three Hebrew children stepping into the fiery furnace. It is Daniel being thrown into the den of lions. It is Elijah on Mount Carmel facing 400 prophets of Baal. It is Stephen being stoned for his faith. It is the Syrophoenician woman pleading for her daughter. It is the "sinful" woman in a Pharisee's house washing Jesus' feet

"Have I not commanded you?"

with expensive perfume applied with her long hair.

To be sure that Joshua got the meaning, God contrasted His command with the opposite. It is a great teaching tool. Things are usually more clearly seen when the opposite is shown. *"Do not be frightened, and do not be dismayed."* I have not personally counted them, but it is said that the words, *Do not fear* or *Do not be afraid* appear exactly 365 times in Scripture—one for every day of the year.

Why the command *to Joshua?* Had he not already, throughout his life near the apex of Israel's leadership, proven that he was loyal, devoted, and brave? Hadn't he withstood the people's rebellion? It couldn't have been easy.

Of course I do not know God's mind, but I know that God never speaks superfluous words. I can imagine some reasons for this command to Joshua.

First of all, Joshua was stepping into Moses' shoes. Oh my! Israel had never had any other leader. Moses had negotiated with Pharaoh the release of the nation from slavery in Egypt. They had left with great riches. He led them for forty years as they passed through the desert. He had been amazingly patient with their almost constant complaints and rebellion. Time and again he had interceded for them with God, sparing their lives. He had given them God's moral law and ceremonial requirements. (Someone has called these the only *revealed* culture ever on earth.) No way could Joshua hope to rise to that standard! Would the people be able to respect and trust him?

Secondly, there was the difficulty of taking the land from its current occupants. The residents of Canaan were very evil in God's sight. They certainly deserved God's judgment, and it was time. Israel would be God's tool to bring that judgment upon evil nations. But they would not go easily. The cities were strong and fortified. The people were, in some cases, mighty. There were giants among them. They were warlike. They were used to fighting to protect their territories. Further, they were settled in. Besides the established cities, they had farms and vineyards. They would defend themselves mightily.

Then there was the relative unpreparedness of God's people. Remember that they were descendants of slaves. They did agricultural work. They did construction work. They did not do war. They didn't have the training or discipline of an organized army! And they didn't have adequate armaments or equipment. They had few weapons of war. When they subsequently took Jericho, the walled city, they did so with torches, pitchers, trumpets, and shouts—some weapons!

The people of God did occasionally have to defend themselves against marauding enemies in the wilderness. In Exodus 17, we read about the time that Amalek came against Israel at Rephidim. Moses commanded Joshua to choose some men to go fight the Amalekites in the valley while he interceded on the mountaintop. Joshua and the Israelites prevailed as Moses held his staff high before God, and Aaron and Hur held his arms aloft when he was too tired to continue—a beautiful picture of effectual prayer and of the fellowship of believers who bear each other's burdens. *And a beautiful statement that Israel's success did not depend upon their superior war machine!*

Finally, perhaps Joshua's biggest challenge was the reluctance of his people to go into Canaan and conquer it. *Reluctance* is too kind a description. They were not only unprepared, they were unconvinced; in some cases, unwilling. Although their rebellious, faithless fathers and mothers died in the wilderness, the children could remember the negative reports from the ten spies. Would it be different this time? (The fact that they did not complete the conquest of Canaan underlines their slowness in following God's design for them.)

Yes, Joshua needed to hear God's command, "Be strong and courageous. . . ." It would take a titanium backbone for Joshua to complete this assignment.

"Be strong. Be courageous. Chin up! Look on the bright side. When the going gets tough, the tough get going. Be happy! Put your brave on!" These are the platitudes, the empty clichés, that we say to each other when faced with difficulty.

Was God appealing to Joshua to "gin up" some inner strength? Was He acting as a divine cheerleader to Joshua, to boost his morale? Of course not. We know that for sure because of what follows the command: "*. . . for the* L*ord* *your God is with you wherever you go.*" It wouldn't be Joshua's strength that would win the day.

It would be God's powerful presence and infinite resources right there with him.

> The LORD is my light and my salvation; whom shall I fear? The LORD is the strength of my life; of whom shall I be afraid?
> (Psalm 27:1)

> "God is our refuge and strength, a very present help in trouble. Therefore we will not fear. . . ."
> (Psalm 46:1,2)

Both of those are followed by descriptions of terrifying circumstances: in one case enemies all around, and in the other catastrophic events in nature—storms, earthquakes and tsunamis.

These words follow the great commission recorded in Matthew 28: "And behold, I am with you always to the end of the age."

Hebrews 13:5,6 tells us, "For he [God] has said, 'I will never leave you nor forsake you.' So we can confidently say, 'The Lord is my helper; I will not fear; what can man do to me?'"

The apostle Paul, after pleading three times for God to remove a painful impediment in his life, heard God say to him, "My grace is sufficient for you, for my power is made perfect in weakness."

God was calling on Joshua to trust Him, to go forward confident in God's ever-present help in every time of need.

I remember the lowest point in my life, when I was so full of grief that I couldn't form a request to God. My prayer as I walked through the house was simply, *"Jesus, Jesus, Jesus, Jesus."* I was utterly weak, broken, emotionally disabled. And yet, I was incredibly strong! As I look back on that period, I wonder how I did what I did. I was both weak and strong at the same time. The weak part was me. The strong part was my Lord who was with me every minute. The words of Psalm 23 became my motto: "The LORD is my Shepherd. I have everything I need."

Three times God commanded Joshua to be strong and courageous. The third time He prefaced it with a question.

"Have I not commanded you?"

The repetition plus the question has the force of emphasis. It is as if God is calling for Joshua's attention, drawing his focus. "Take this seriously, Joshua."

Could it be a gentle rebuke? *Or* maybe a sweet accommodation to the human tendency to need to hear important things repeated?

In any case, Joshua needed to hear the command again. We know from the remainder of the book of Joshua that he indeed persevered in strength and courage, fortified by his experience of the presence and power of God always with him.

The book closes with a memorable exchange between Joshua and the elders of Israel. Joshua knows that his death is near. He recaps for the elders the history of the nation, and then calls on them to choose. Not all of the idol gods of the heathen nations in Canaan have been eliminated. There will still be temptations to idolatry. Joshua famously said, ". . .choose you this day whom you will serve, whether the gods your fathers served. . .or the gods of the Amorites in whose land you dwell, *but as for me and my house, we will serve the* Lord" (Joshua 24:15).

And that says it all.

"Have I not commanded you?"

❖

"Have I not commanded you?"

For Further Thought

Isaiah 43:1–7
Matthew 10:26–31
Ephesians 6:10–20
2 Timothy 1:7

❖

9

"How long will you grieve over Saul?"

1 SAMUEL 16:1

The Lord said to Samuel, "How long will you grieve over Saul, since I have rejected him from being king over Israel? Fill your horn with oil, and go. I will send you to Jesse the Bethlehemite, for I have provided for myself a king among his sons."

When one thinks of the great Bible stories of the Old Testament and their heroes, the name Samuel doesn't usually come to mind. Although he played a prominent role in Israel's history, there is no single event in his life that rivals stories like Noah and the ark, Jonah and the great fish, or Daniel in the lions' den. His was a life of quiet faithfulness.

Samuel, the last judge of Israel, bridged the period from the judges to King David, who, with his son King Solomon, reigned at the apex of Israel's history, the height of its glory. His ministry spanned nearly fifty years.

Samuel wore many hats. Although he is usually referred to as a prophet, he is the only person in Scripture, other than Jesus Christ, who was a judge, a priest, *and* a prophet.

Someone has ruefully commented that Samuel is also the only "ghost" in the Old Testament! King Saul repeatedly preferred his own wisdom over God's, and therefore lost God's guidance. Near the end of his life, directionless, threatened by the Philistine army, desperate, he sought out a medium, the widow of Endor, and asked her to conjure up Samuel from beyond the grave, which she did. Predictably, Samuel's words to Saul were not comforting! But I am getting ahead of the story.

To say that Samuel's childhood was unique is an understatement! His mother, Hannah, was at first unable to have children. She pled with God for a child, promising that she would give such child to God. God heard her passionate prayers, and she bore a son and named him *Samuel* which means *heard of God*. When he was weaned, she brought him and presented him to Eli, the priest, for service in the tabernacle, fulfilling her pledge.

It was there, in the middle of the night, that the boy Samuel heard the voice of God calling to him by name. Repeatedly mistaking God's voice for Eli's, Samuel eventually, upon Eli's advice, answered, "Speak, for your servant hears." Little did he know what he would hear!

Samuel's initial obedience to the voice of God set the course of his whole life. That night God had told Samuel that He was about to punish the house of Eli for years of priestly misconduct on the part of his sons, Hophni and Phinehas. Imagine how hard it must have been for Samuel to give this message to Eli! But he did, and that faithfulness to God—and man—characterized the remainder of his long life.

Most of the book of 1 Samuel is a history of the first two kings of Israel, Saul and David, but actually, Samuel was an old man before he ever heard of Saul. He spent the majority of his life as a circuit judge traveling among the tribes of Israel and adjudicating their problems. The Bible gives scant details concerning this part of Samuel's life.

As an old man, he evidently desired to step back somewhat from his demanding schedule, so he conferred judgeships on his sons, Joel and Abijah. It is curious, at least, that Samuel's sons were no better than Eli's sons! Joel and Abijah were corrupt—greedy for money, and willing to pervert justice to get it. As a consequence, the elders of Israel, noting that Samuel was old and his sons unfit, requested a king to rule over them. This did not please Samuel, who foresaw all the complications a king would bring to the nation.

He also felt it as a rejection of his long ministry to the nation. We know that because he took his wounds to the Lord in prayer, and God answered him, ". . .they have not rejected you, but they have rejected me from being king over them" (1 Samuel 8:7).

God counseled Samuel to give them a king, but not before warning them how a king would negatively affect their lives. This Samuel did, and it wasn't long before God brought Saul to Samuel and revealed to him that this tall, handsome man was the one to anoint as Israel's first king—a momentous event.

Saul began his reign in humility, but soon became enamored of his own position. His ego got the best of him, and he began to make decisions contrary to what God had commanded him. He exalted his own wisdom over God's, and, when confronted, showed no remorse, but rather defended his actions.

"How long will you grieve over Saul?"

Finally, Samuel addressed Saul in some of the most memorable words in all of Scripture:

> Has the LORD as great delight in burnt offerings and sacrifices,
> as in obeying the voice of the LORD?
> Behold, to obey is better than sacrifice, and to learn than the fat of rams. . .
> Because you have rejected the word of the LORD,
> He has also rejected you from being King.
> (1 Samuel 15:22–23)

Chapter 15 of 1 Samuel ends with hard words: "And Samuel did not see Saul again until the day of his death, but Samuel grieved over Saul. And the LORD regretted that He had made Saul king over Israel."

> *"How long will you grieve over Saul, since I have rejected him from being king over Israel?"*

This question, embodying a rebuke and a challenge, calls for consideration. Implied is that some time has passed since Saul's rejection. God was finished with Saul, but he was *not finished* with Samuel. Samuel still had work to do; another assignment was waiting.

(The question here reminds me of the question asked of the disciples by the angels attending Jesus' ascension, "Men of Galilee, why do you stand looking into heaven?" Then, the assurance that the *same* Jesus would return.)

We know from elsewhere in Scripture that God was not prohibiting grief itself. Ecclesiastes 3:4 states that there is a time to weep, a time to mourn. Jesus begins His famous Sermon on the Mount proclaiming blessing upon those who mourn. In Romans 12:15 we are counseled to "weep with those who weep." Elsewhere in Scripture, mourning is an important step in repentance. For sure, in this fallen world, there are circumstances that rightly call for mourning. Remember, *Jesus wept!*

Jeremiah is called "the weeping prophet." He prophesied during a very dark period, when Israel was destroyed by the Babylonian empire. The book that follows Jeremiah, Lamentations, is a book full of mourning. It is instructive that it is included in Holy Scripture.

The fact that Samuel grieved endears him to me. It shows me his deep sensitivity and compassion.

The problem with Samuel's grief is clearly shown in the second half of God's question: "...since I have rejected him..." It wasn't the grief itself. It seems that Samuel was "stuck." His grief, stemming from his keen disappointment in Saul, kept him from moving forward with God's plan, doing what God had called him to do. God had moved on. Samuel had not. Samuel was not on the same page as God. The Pillar of Cloud and Pillar of Fire were moving. Samuel was not following. The operative words are "How long..."

Did Samuel take Saul's failure personally? People disappoint. It is a constant in life. Even the great and godly King David had a grievous moral failure during his reign. Sometimes the betrayal is so deeply wounding that it is hard for one to move forward.

Think of it. Samuel hadn't wanted a king to begin with. He who had faithfully shepherded Israel for over forty years had a lot invested in the spiritual prosperity of the nation. He longed for the best for them. With a heavy heart, he obeyed God and anointed Saul king. After doing so, he desperately wanted Saul to be a good king, a great leader. Yes, it was personal for Samuel. Yes, his broken heart was exposed.

God had rejected Saul. Samuel had not. Remember that Samuel had failed to properly restrain his corrupt sons. Was he also, perhaps, too passive, too lenient with Saul's disobedience? Or conversely, was Samuel unable to forgive Saul? Often the two—love and anger—go hand in hand.

God was calling Samuel to "forget what lies behind and strain forward to what lies ahead" (Philippians 3:13). There was a teenage lad, a boy shepherd, a young musician and poet, a young man after God's own heart, unaware of God's call on his life.

> *"How long will you grieve over Saul, since I have rejected him from being king over Israel?"*

Following this question, God went on to instruct Samuel to anoint a future king from among the sons of Jesse, the Bethlehemite. Samuel then voiced another emotion—fear. "If Saul hears it, he will kill me." Saul, after all, was king. He had all the resources of the nation. Samuel could be crushed.

What is the bottom line here? It is the same as it always is—an issue of the heart. "Keep your heart with all vigilance for from it flow the springs of life" (Proverbs 4:23). Samuel was a loyal, devoted servant of God, but at this moment in his life, sorrow, disappointment, and fear ruled his heart.

"No! No. . .no. . .no. . ." I didn't utter the word aloud, but my heart whispered it urgently in my head. What God had put on my plate, I emphatically did not want. The future was black. I had no peace. In His time, my rescuing Redeemer subdued my will and I eventually found contentment, even joy in following His plan.

"How long will you grieve over Saul, since I have rejected him from being king over Israel?"

Samuel, the kind, faithful old man, took God's rebuke. He trusted God and headed to Jesse's place.

"How long will you grieve over_____?"

❖

For Further Thought

Luke 9:57–62

Luke 10:16

2 Corinthians 2:14–17

❖

10

"What are you doing here, Elijah?"

1 KINGS 19:13

And when Elijah heard it, he wrapped his face in his cloak and went out and stood at the entrance of the cave. And behold, there came a voice to him and said, "What are you doing here, Elijah?"

Who can forget the scene on Mount Carmel? The prophets of Baal, four hundred fifty of them, remonstrating with their god for fire from the sky to burn up the offering. When Baal doesn't answer, increasingly desperate, they cry louder, dancing around the altar, even cutting themselves, all to no avail. Then Elijah, after soaking the altar and surrounding ground with water, prays a simple prayer to the God of Abraham, Isaac, and Jacob, and fire falls from heaven and consumes the offering. A drama for the ages!

Talk about the road less traveled. . . Elijah is a larger-than-life character, a prophet who demonstrated, as few did, the power of Jehovah. Unlike most of the Old Testament prophets, there is no book of the Bible named after Elijah, yet he is so unique in his service to God and the nation that he is given a place of prominence in Scripture, even in the life of Jesus Christ, most notably on the Mount of Transfiguration. The New Testament records that there he appeared with Moses, as Jesus is glorified in front of the disciples Peter, James, and John. Only two Old Testament prophets and God incarnate in the person of Jesus Christ—rarified air, rarified company.

As if to put an exclamation point on Elijah's prophetic stature, at the end of his life, God lowers a chariot from heaven and takes Elijah up to Himself in it, so that Elijah does not experience death—a special transport, a divine limousine!

The Bible tells us nothing of Elijah's birth, childhood, or youth. It is as if he came on the scene the same way he left the scene! We are simply told that he was a Tishbite, of the city of Tishbe in Gilead. That is all we know of his origins. We first hear of him when he takes a message from God to King Ahab.

And what a message it was! "As the LORD of Israel lives, before whom I stand, there shall be neither dew nor rain these years, except by my word" (1 Kings 17: 1).

Ahab, king of Israel, was a very evil leader. We are introduced to him this way:

> ...Ahab the son of Omri began to reign over Israel, and Ahab the son of Omri reigned over Israel in Samaria twenty-two years. And Ahab the son of Omri did evil in the sight of the LORD, more than all who were before him.
> (1 Kings 16:29, 30)

Then we are told that (as if it hadn't been enough that he copied the sins of Jeroboam) he took Jezebel, a Sidonian (an alien to Israel) to be his wife. God had forbidden His people to intermarry with the idolatrous nations surrounding them. Further, Ahab adopted the religion of his new wife, a devotee of Baal, demonstrating the very reason God gave for banning such unions. He went on to promote the worship of Baal to the extent of erecting a shrine to that heathen idol.

God was ready to move against Ahab and the nation that was rapidly following his example. No rain. Not even any dew. For a very long time. Drought would inevitably lead to famine.

And then the spotlight turns from Ahab to Elijah. And what follows is a tender account of the love of God for His servant. "The LORD is my Shepherd, I shall not want" (Psalm 23:1). As the nation was descending into poverty and deprivation—no water, no food—God was providing for Elijah. First, He *hid* Elijah. Surely, as shortages became the norm in Israel, Ahab would be after Elijah's hide!

Then God *fed* Elijah. He sent him east over the Jordan River (perhaps beyond the reach of Ahab?) to camp near a brook. As we shall see even more profoundly later in our story, God is Lord over creation, and all of the natural world obeys Him. In this case, ravens were commanded by God to feed Elijah, and sure enough, each morning and each evening, ravens brought him bread and meat in their beaks, dropping his meal before him. Wait a minute! Ravens are carnivorous. Ravens are predatory. And this was a drought. This was severe famine. Nevertheless, ravens indeed fed Elijah. I am in awe of the command of God over nature. And I am

"What are you doing here, Elijah?"

deeply touched by the love of God for His prophet.

But the story goes from being amazing to being miraculous. The brook eventually dried up. So God sent Elijah to the village of Zeraphath in Sidon. Just as He had commanded the ravens, God also commanded a widow in Zeraphath to feed Elijah.

It is one thing for God to command animals against their nature. It is a whole other thing to command a human being against reason. A widow...a child...a famine...survival...or not. A precious widow was gathering sticks to make a fire over which to prepare some unleavened bread. She had so little flour, so little oil; this was to be their last meal. She had become reconciled to their death. She believed in the sovereign providence of God. She did not fear death, for she was confident of her place in the "house of the LORD forever." Yet surely she was sad for her child. Starvation, after all, is a terrible way to die.

It was unthinkable to be asked to feed Elijah the last bit of food she had, therefore hastening the starvation of herself and her son. How could he ask such a thing of her? But God had commanded her to feed Elijah, and obey she did. Her deep faith made it possible for her to do the impossible—impossible because what mother could possibly do this?

God not only fed Elijah; He also daily increased the flour and oil supply, so that the widow and her son ate plenty until the drought was over.

The son died anyway. The widow's faith was severely tested, but God used Elijah to raise the boy from the dead. What a story this woman had to tell!

I can't help but note that this faithful widow was a Sidonian, as was Jezebel. But what a contrast in worship and in character. It demonstrates that the issue is the orientation of the heart, not the place or the culture surrounding it.

And then the scene changes to the palace. There Ahab told the queen that after Elijah embarrassed all the prophets of Baal by calling fire from heaven at God's command, he then killed them all. God has a zero tolerance for idolatry!

Jezebel was hopping mad. She was devoted to Baal. Those priests of Baal were her priests. She had suffered enough during the drought and famine. Now this... so she sent a messenger to

Elijah to tell him that she vowed to her gods to kill him, and to accomplish it within twenty-four hours.

1 Kings 19:3 tells us "Then he was afraid and . . .ran for his life. . ." Adrenalin propelled Elijah to run from Jezreel to Beersheba, a distance of approximately a hundred miles! Then, leaving his servant in Beersheba, he traveled another day's journey into the wilderness. When he finally came to rest, he prayed that God would take away his life. It seems he wanted to die, but not by the hand of Jezebel!

Remarkably, God did not chide Elijah for his overwhelming discouragement, for his inappropriate request. Oh, the deep, deep love of Jesus! Twice an angel woke Elijah from sleep and served him a hot meal. God knows that often what a discouraged servant of His needs is not a scolding or a lecture, but rather some lovingkindness.

"What are you doing here, Elijah?"

Elijah continued to put distance between himself and Queen Jezebel. He traveled south, forty days and forty nights to Horeb, the mountain of God, of which Sinai is a part. There he made a camp in a cave. Running. . .hiding. . .but just as the Lord followed Hagar into the desert, so the Lord followed Elijah into the mountains, into a cave. And the Lord had a question for Elijah:

"What are you doing here, Elijah?"

Elijah answered,

> I have been very jealous for the LORD, the God of hosts. For the people of Israel have forsaken your covenant, thrown down your altars, and killed your prophets with the sword, and I, even I only, am left, and they seek my life, to take it away.
> (1 Kings 19:14)

"It's so unfair! I, Elijah, have been faithful and fervent for You, Lord of the heavenly armies. The people have rebelled against

You in every way. And I am being hunted like an animal! I don't deserve this!"

Surely God knew what Elijah was doing hundreds of miles from Mt. Carmel. Elijah's answer was not honest. It was defensive. It was self-righteous. Elijah was aggrieved. It wasn't supposed to come to this—a great prophet alone in a mountain cave trembling with fear of an angry queen.

Really, Elijah was mad at God. Really, he was accusing God. He knew full well that God controls all the events of our lives. God had let him down big time. Where was God over the past month when Jezebel's minions were chasing after Elijah?

In my youth and naivety I thought that, if I loved God and served Him to the best of my ability, nothing bad would ever happen to me—well, at least nothing seriously bad. Then when my life seemed reduced to ashes, I accused God. I was sure that He had not kept His promises to me. Where was protection? Where was abundant life? Where were goodness and mercy, supposed to be following me? Where were answered prayers?

Surprisingly, God did not argue with Elijah or point out his misconceptions. He simply commanded him to go outside the cave and stand on the mountain before the Lord.

There followed a spectacular display of power. First there was a mighty cyclone, so strong that the mountains were torn and huge rocks broken into pieces. That was only the beginning. Next came an earthquake, and after that fire from heaven. God could have shouted to Elijah from the center of the storm, the earthquake, or the fire. But He didn't. Instead, there came to Elijah's ears a low whisper. Hearing it, he grabbed his cloak and stood at the entrance to the cave. Then the voice asked the question again.

"What are you doing here, Elijah?"

It is said correctly that if you want someone to pay attention to what you say, speak in a whisper. There is a difference between hearing and listening. We constantly hear noise all around us. Most of the time we tune it out. But we must *listen* to a whisper. We must focus our attention if we are to understand a whisper. It is a technique used by teachers of very young children.

Also, words of love and caring are not usually shouted. Words of endearment are whispered. Think of lovers sitting close, exchanging loving expressions. Think of a mother rocking her infant, whispering loving sentiments in his ear.

"What are you doing here, Elijah?"

God did not scold Elijah. Even after Elijah repeated his self-pitying defense, God did not rebuke him. No doubt, later Elijah would think back on the demonstration of power he experienced on the mountain, and realize that he had no need to fear Jezebel. She could threaten a prophet. She could command armies. She could muster horses and chariots. She could not command the forces of creation. She could not tell wind what to do. She could not maneuver tectonic plates under the surface of the earth. She could not call down fire from heaven any more than her phony prophets could.

Oh, Elijah, you needn't have been afraid of Jezebel. Surely you see that now.

And so, God simply gave Elijah a series of new assignments: "Enough of running away. Enough of self-pity. Time to get on with the work I have given you to do, Elijah. And just so you know, I have seven thousand devoted followers who have not bowed to Baal!"

"What are you doing here, Elijah?"

❖

"What are you doing here, Elijah?"

For Further Thought

Psalm 27:1–14

Psalm 56:1–13

Matthew 5:10–15

❖

11

"Should I not pity Nineveh?"

JONAH 4:11

"And should not I pity Nineveh, that great city, in which there are more than 120,000 persons who do not know their right hand from their left, and also much cattle?"

This is the last verse of the book of Jonah, and it summarizes the theme of the book of Jonah. Because the story of Jonah being swallowed by, and then hosted by, a large fish is so compelling, it is the single thing most people know about the book of Jonah. It is a significant story, but there is so much more to the overall message of the book.

Jonah is one of the minor prophets, and the book that bears his name is a small book—four short chapters. The theme of the book is actually the theme of all of Scripture, encompassing the whole world, and as old as its creation. In the question above, God asks, "And should not I pity. . ." The word *pity* is otherwise translated *compassion*. "And should I not have compassion. . ." This is the theme of the book of Jonah—the compassion of God—both for Nineveh and for Jonah.

The compassion of God juxtaposed against the anger of the prophet is powerfully portrayed. God is the protagonist and Jonah the antagonist. We could call it "Jonah, the angry prophet and Jehovah, the merciful God." God had compassion on Jonah and He had compassion on Nineveh. God rescued Jonah and He rescued Nineveh. Nineveh repented. Jonah did not. Yes, Jonah, after his sojourn in the belly of a fish, did turn around and go to Nineveh after all, and preached there. But his "repentance" was superficial. At the end of the book he is still angry. The reason for his original avoidance of Nineveh remained.

Before delving into the story of Jonah and Nineveh, a few words about the historical aspect of the book of Jonah: Because the account of Jonah surviving the stomach, not to mention the teeth, of a large fish is so amazing, even fantastic, skeptics tend to think of it as a fairy tale, a work of fiction. But Scriptures outside of the book of Jonah prove otherwise. 1 Kings 14:23 tells us that Jeroboam was king when Jonah prophesied, clearly setting Jonah's life and ministry in historical context. Even more convincing, in Matthew 12:39–41, Jesus compared Himself to Jonah, and compared Nineveh's response to Jonah's preaching to the response of His audience to His preaching.

The story begins with God directing Jonah to go to Nineveh, and "call out against it." Nineveh had become an evil city, and God wanted Jonah to warn its citizens of coming judgment if they did not repent. (The Bible does not detail the sins of Nineveh, but extra-biblical historians note violence, sexual orgies, and political and financial corruption.)

Jonah would have none of this mission. He, instead, went the other way, putting as much distance as he could between himself and Nineveh. Why?

Jonah was a preacher. Wouldn't he welcome an assignment to preach in a large metropolitan area? Any place but Nineveh!

Nineveh was the capital of Assyria. It was not part of God's chosen nation, Israel. It was a Gentile city. Ninevites were foreigners. Furthermore, Assyria had positioned itself against Israel, repeatedly picking a fight with its neighbor Israel, and threatening to destroy it, which ultimately took place. Nineveh was the enemy.

Why would God send Jonah *there*? The psalmist says it so well:

> The LORD is merciful and gracious, slow to anger and abounding in steadfast love. . .He does not deal with us according to our sins, nor repay us according to our iniquities, for as high as the heavens are above the earth, so great is his steadfast love toward those who fear him. . .As a father shows compassion on his children, so the LORD shows compassion to those who fear him. . . .
> (Psalm 103:8–13)

The Scriptures teach us that God chose the nation Israel, named after the second son of Isaac, otherwise known as Jacob, the father of the twelve tribes. His purpose was not to bless them alone, but to bless the whole world through them. God promised Abraham not only that he would be the father of a great nation, but that through that nation, the whole world would be blessed.

Throughout the Bible, God's love for the whole world is clearly seen. "For God so loved *the world* that He gave His only Son. . ." (John 3:16). One of the last things Jesus did before leaving this world to ascend back into heaven was to commission His disciples to "Go. . .and make disciples of *all nations*. . . ." (Matthew 28:19).

"Should not I pity Nineveh?"

"And should not I pity Nineveh, that great city, in which there are more than 120,000 persons who do not know their right hand from their left, and also much cattle?"

To take up the story, Jonah found a ship headed for Tarshish, the opposite direction from Nineveh, "away from the presence of the LORD." Jonah not only avoided Nineveh; he fled from God. Jonah, the angry prophet—angry that God would expect him to do *anything* to help Nineveh. No way!

God always has the last word. He, who controls all of creation, "hurled a great wind upon the sea." The storm was so fierce that the ship began to break up and seasoned sailors feared for their lives, so much so that they threw overboard the cargo they had been hauling. Finally, frantic, they roughly awakened a napping Jonah, begging him to call out on his god to save them all.

Little by little, Jonah's story emerged—how he was a Hebrew and was fleeing from the presence of his God, Jehovah. As the sea grew yet more tempestuous, the sailors inquired of Jonah what they could do to make the storm abate. Jonah directed them to cast him into the stormy sea, but they did not want to do that. Instead, they redoubled their efforts to row hard toward land, but they couldn't make any progress. Exhausted and desperate, they threw Jonah overboard, all the while asking God's forgiveness for doing so.

Every Sunday school child knows what happened next. God had prepared a very large fish to swallow Jonah whole. This is sometimes portrayed as a punishment, but really it was a rescue. Apart from the fish's swallowing Jonah, he surely would have drowned.

During three uneasy days and nights in the belly of the fish, Jonah prayed mightily. It was a prayer of thanksgiving for being rescued from drowning, ". . .the flood surrounded me; all your waves and your billows passed over me. . . . The waters closed in over me to take my life; the deep surrounded me; weeds were wrapped about my head at the roots of the mountains. I went down to the land whose bars closed upon me forever; yet you brought up my life from the pit, O LORD my God" (Jonah 2:3–6).

"And should not I pity Nineveh, that great city, in which there are more than 120,000 persons who do not know their right hand from their left, and also much cattle?"

"Then the word of the LORD came to Jonah the second time. . . ." Again, the compassionate God—after saving Jonah's life—gives him a second opportunity to fulfill his commission. He doesn't deal with us as our sins deserve. He is slow to anger and abounding in love.

So Jonah shuffled off to Nineveh. He definitely wasn't thrilled to be going there. But what else could he do after God had so spectacularly rescued him from death in deep waters?

He preached God's message of judgment, and Nineveh repented. No, not as a whole, but "Let *everyone* turn from his evil way and from the violence that is in his hands" (Jonah 3:8).

"When God saw what they did, how they turned from their evil way, God relented of the disaster that he had said he would do to them, and he did not do it" (Jonah 3:10).

"But it displeased Jonah exceedingly, and he was angry" (Jonah 4:1). He was the only preacher ever to be irritated by his success!

"And should not I pity Nineveh, that great city, in which there are more than 120,000 persons who do not know their right hand from their left, and also much cattle?"

How could God forgive Nineveh? After all the Assyrians had done to Israel over the years. . . They deserved God's wrath and condemnation. This was a gross injustice! How could Nineveh go free? Jonah argued with God.

> O LORD, is not this what I said when I was yet in my country? That is why I made haste to flee to Tarshish; for I knew that you are a gracious God and merciful, slow to anger and abounding in steadfast love. . . .
> (Jonah 4:2)

Jonah actually admitted that he was unlike God. God was merciful. Jonah was not. Jonah ran away from Nineveh. God ran toward Nineveh. Jonah rejoiced in justice. Period. God rejoices in mercy.

Assyria was the enemy. Nineveh was evil. Jonah was offended. Jonah wanted vengeance. Jonah was upset not by God's wrath and judgment. He was upset by God's compassion!

It reminds me of the parable Jesus taught about forgiveness. A man owed a huge debt that he could not possibly ever pay. He was an immediate candidate for debtors' prison—he and his wife and children. His master, to whom the debt was owed, forgave the debt. Then he who was forgiven found a man who owed him but a pittance, grabbed him by the throat, hauled him into court and had him imprisoned until he paid up.

Jonah had been forgiven for his reckless flight to Tarshish. He had defied God. Nevertheless, God rescued him from the storm, and gave him a second chance to fulfill his assignment and go to Nineveh. Gratitude and humility should have motivated him to feel mercy for the Ninevites and welcome their repentance. "And should not you have had mercy. . . as I had mercy on you?" (Matthew 18:33)

Jesus said, "Love your enemies and pray for those who persecute you, so that you may be sons of your Father who is in heaven" (Matthew 5:44, 45). This command humbles me. There are many "religious" duties that I do not find difficult. I can go to church. I can read the Bible. I can pray. There are other spiritual disciplines that are difficult, but not impossible. *This* command to love my enemies leaves me undone. It is impossible apart from God's grace working mightily in me. Faced with this command, I flee to Christ for help. I flee to the cross for forgiveness and transformation for my hard heart.

Neither could Jonah forgive his enemies. In fact, he was so angry with God for sparing Nineveh its deserved punishment that he asked God to take his life. He didn't want to live in the same world as a forgiven, rescued, restored Nineveh!

Jesus vividly pictured the love and compassion of God in the parable of the prodigal son. Betrayed, disrespected, and devalued, the Father nevertheless daily searched the horizon for a sign that his son was returning. When he saw the first tiny image of his son on the distant road, he unceremoniously hiked up his robe and literally ran to meet his son. He was impatient with his son's confession, as he couldn't wait to welcome him back with hugs and kisses and gifts and a party! This is but a small representation of the compassion of God.

How does God look at you? He looks at you with love and compassion.

Next, God taught Jonah by using a live object lesson. Jonah had gone outside the city and made a small shelter for himself where he could watch what would happen with the city. Maybe God would yet bring the disaster that they deserved. God used a large vine to reveal truth to Jonah. God caused the vine to grow up and shade Jonah, which made Jonah glad. Then God sent a worm to eat the vine and wither it. He also sent a scorching wind and sun. Jonah was so angry that again he prayed to die.

Then came the dagger to the heart of an angry prophet. God pointed out that Jonah cared more for a cheap plant which he did not sow nor tend, than he cared for a large population in a city—120,000 persons who do not know their right hand from their left (a reference to young children, and therefore perhaps an indication that the population was actually much larger) and also much cattle. The compassion of God even extends to animals!

And so ends the book of Jonah. We do not know if Jonah ever repented of his anger.

An angry prophet. A compassionate God.

> Oh, Lord, I am so thankful for Your love and compassion. I owed a debt I could not pay. Jesus paid it all. I deserved Your wrath. I received Your grace. Forgive me, Lord, for the times I want vengeance. Forgive me for holding grudges. Forgive me for not readily forgiving others. Forgive me for not loving my enemies. Make me like You, Lord. In Jesus' Name. Amen.

> *"And should not I pity Nineveh, that great city, in which there are more than 120,000 persons who do not know their right hand from their left, and also much cattle?"*

❖

"Should I not pity Nineveh?"

For Further Thought

Psalm 103:8–13
Isaiah 54:8
Luke 15:11–32

❖

12

"Do you want to be healed?"

JOHN 5:6

When Jesus saw him lying there and knew that he had already been there a long time, he said to him, "Do you want to be healed?"

It was the Feast of the Passover and Jerusalem was crowded with pilgrims from all around the country and beyond. Surely the tumult of the bustling city reached the ears of a man lying by a pool near the famous Sheep Gate. But he would not be celebrating the Passover. He was not lying by the pool because he was relaxing. He was lying by the pool because he was an invalid. He was disabled. He could not walk.

The pool was named Bethesda, and ancient tradition tells us, and the New King James Version of this passage includes, that this man was "waiting for the moving of the water, for an angel of the Lord went down at certain seasons into the pool, and stirred the water. Whoever stepped in first after the stirring of the water was healed of whatever disease he had." The man in question was not the only one lying by the pool. In fact, Scripture tells us that a multitude of the blind, the lame, and the paralyzed were reclining at the pool waiting for the miracle cure to their ailment.

An observant Jew, Jesus was also in Jerusalem for the Passover Feast, and He passed by the pool of Bethesda. Out of the multitude, He zeroed in on this man. He knew this man! This man had been an invalid for thirty-eight years! How many of those years had he spent lying by this pool?

"Do you want to be healed?"

The sick man answered him "Sir, I have no one to put me into the pool when the water is stirred up, and while I am going, another steps down before me" (John 5:7).

Jesus' question "Do you want to be healed?" is a curious one. It seems (no disrespect intended) to be a silly question. Really, Jesus? This man has been an invalid for thirty-eight years. Isn't it obvious that his existence is very limited both in scope and duration? Not to mention the fact that he was lying by a pool known for containing healing waters. Of course he wants to be healed!

It reminds me of a similar incident, also recorded in the Gospels. Just outside of Jericho, two blind men sitting by the side of the road drew Jesus' attention. Despite the crowd surrounding Jesus as He passed by them, the blind men called out. "Lord, have mercy on us, Son of David!" (Matthew 20:30).

Blind beggars sitting by the road didn't receive much consideration. The crowd admonished them to be quiet. That just made them call out louder for mercy. Then Jesus stopped and asked them a similarly quizzical question: "What do you want me to do for you?" Isn't it obvious? These men were humiliated on a daily basis. They were dirty, hungry, ragged beggars all because they were blind. They answered as one would expect, "Lord, let our eyes be opened" (Matthew 20:33).

But why the questions—to them and to the man by the pool?

Jesus, who is God, does not ask stupid questions. These are important questions. They drill down into the souls of these men.

"Do you want to be healed?"

The answer is not so obvious as it seems at first. Why wouldn't a person want to be healed? First of all, this man had been by the pool for years. His life was predictable. Every day, a friend or family member brought him to the pool where he lay waiting. It was not a good life by any stretch, but it was a life he was used to. In a sense, it was his comfort zone.

Secondly, to be well would mean a total transformation in his life. Yes, a wonderful transformation, but, wait—a scary transformation. A healthy life would mean taking all the responsibilities of a grown man in society. It would mean working, caring for family members, participating in all aspects of the worship of Jehovah, providing for his own needs for food, shelter, and clothing—responsibilities that can be very intimidating, especially for someone who has never assumed them.

It is common knowledge that the greatest challenge in addressing alcoholics and addicts of all kinds is their reluctance to change. On one level they want to get better, but on another they fear losing the "crutch" that their addiction has become. They fear the burden of taking responsibility as a healthy adult, and doing so without self-medication.

Humans have the capacity to acclimate to almost any circumstance over time. We can adjust. We can make the best of very negative living conditions. We can become content with situations that should not be acceptable—like spending one's days lying by a pool amid a group of similarly challenged people.

It is said that a large reason for the high recidivism rate among the prison population is the inability of parolees to acclimate to life on the outside. Prison may be a horrible place to live, but it is a predictable life. There are three meals a day, a bed, a routine. It is an uncomfortable comfortableness. To be on the outside is to face the bewildering array of choices and responsibilities. It is to face the need to provide for oneself the basic needs. For many, it is too much to handle.

"Do you want to be healed?"

Really?

Our man at the pool *wanted* to be healed. It is interesting that the man did not ask for healing, but Jesus knew his heart. No doubt that is why Jesus was drawn to him in the first place. Yes, it comes down to the heart.

There are uncountable numbers of people in this world who are suffering in a variety of ways—guilt for past indiscretions, broken relationships, disappointed dreams, addictions, financial struggles—even poverty—sickness, and on and on. But they are not ready to be healed by Christ.

Rescue means change, and change is one of the costliest things in the universe. People resist change. It demands a great deal of us. It is easier to remain in the familiar situation.

The first step is to move beyond the present position. Notice that Jesus didn't reach down, lift the man up, and carry him home. Instead, Jesus gave him a series of commands. "Jesus said to him, 'Get up, take up your bed, and walk.'" (John 5:8).

Hold on! That is exactly what this man could not do! If he could have done those things, he would not have been lying for years by this pool.

His obedience to these three commands demonstrated his

That's a Good Question

faith. Trying to get up could have caused him embarrassment and crushing disappointment if he failed to do so. His effort to get up, in spite of that risk, showed that he believed that he was healed. And sure enough, he rose, took up his bed, and walked home. Can you imagine the reaction of his family as they caught sight of him walking toward their home?

But wait, this is not the end of the story. The day this healing happened was the Sabbath. The Jews (Scripture does not specify *which* Jews) saw the man and informed him that it was unlawful to carry his bed on the Sabbath. The man replied that the one who healed him directed him to pick up his bed and walk.

Of course, the legalistic, exacting Jews wanted to know who gave such an unlawful directive. But the healed man replied that he did not know. As usual, Jesus had immediately withdrawn and melted into the crowd milling around Jerusalem during the Passover. Jesus often instructed those he healed to keep the miracle quiet. Why?

Reluctant to work a miracle at the wedding feast at Cana when they ran out of wine, Jesus said to His inquiring mother, "My hour has not yet come" (John 2:4). Throughout the Gospels, it is clear that Jesus did not come to earth to be a hero. He did not come to become a celebrity. He refused to involve Himself in political matters even though His nation was in captivity to the Roman Empire. Jesus came for one reason only—to die. He came as the sacrificial lamb to be slaughtered for the sins of the world. Therefore, even when His great compassion for suffering people drove Him to perform a miracle, as in this case, Jesus kept a low profile. Jesus' "hour" to be glorified would come much later—on the Mount of Transfiguration, at the Resurrection and Ascension, and ultimately when He comes again in power and great glory.

And then something very precious took place. John 5:14 simply states, "Afterward Jesus found [the healed man] in the temple." Was this a coincidental meeting? I think not. The word *found* indicates that Jesus was looking for the man. Oh, the deep, deep love of Jesus. He wasn't finished with this man, because spiritual healing is always far more important than physical healing. The soul lives forever. This mortal body does not.

Jesus addressed him: "See, you are well. Sin no more, that

nothing worse may happen to you." This was not a threat. Rather it was a loving warning. What could be worse than being an invalid for thirty-eight years? What could be worse than spending one's days lying by a pool, waiting for help? At another time, Jesus said, "For what will it profit a man if he gains the whole world and forfeits his life?" Some translations read *soul* for *life*. Losing one's soul is so much more grave than losing one's life.

"Sin no more, that nothing worse. . . ." Sin has consequences. Sin always hurts. The consequences can be experienced in inner conflict, damaged relationships, broken health, failed endeavors, unrealized potential, and most important of all, distance from God, even eternal damnation. *Worse?*

"Do you want to be healed?"

Are you content? Have you become too accustomed to your shortcomings? Are you satisfied with your current level of spiritual discipline, Bible study, prayer, and integrity in relationships?

To be healed spiritually means to leave your spiritual comfort zone, your familiar sins. It means to pursue God with all your heart.

It also means living in the embrace of the eternal, infinite God who loves you profoundly. Countless followers of Jesus down through the ages and presently would testify that it is so worth giving up the whole world to obtain.

"Do you want to be healed?"

❖

For Further Thought

Matthew 4:18–22
Luke 19:1–10
Philippians 3:4–11

❖

13

"Do you see this woman?"

LUKE 7:44

Then turning toward the woman he said to Simon, "Do you see this woman? I entered your house; you gave me no water for my feet, but she has wet my feet with her tears and wiped them with her hair."

Between "you" and "this woman" lay a huge chasm. Two people could not be more different. The contrast between them is sharply on display in this story.

Jesus addressed this question to Simon, a rich, well-connected Pharisee, a member of the religious intelligentsia of his day. He represented success, authority, respect, status. He was "you" in the question.

"This woman..." The fact that her name is not given is reflective of her position among her peers. Women in general were considered less important in the patriarchal society of Jesus' day. But *this* woman. Oh, my. She was a woman of ill-repute. She was a sinner, morally fallen, a prostitute. She was a shame, a scandal, a woman of the night, one to be hidden, invisible, a woman to be ignored—and when she couldn't be ignored, despised—well, the opposite kind of person from Simon, the Pharisee.

After years of plying her trade, she was haggard, dissipated, used up, no longer beautiful or desirable, if ever she had been. Today she might be called a "low life." Ouch.

However, there was an even bigger contrast between these two, Simon and the woman. The woman loved Jesus. Simon did not.

"Do you see this woman?"

To put the question in context is to understand it. Simon invited Jesus to dinner at his home. Why? It was a pretty common understanding that the Pharisees were not fans of Jesus. Perhaps Simon was simply curious. Maybe he wanted to "pick Jesus' brain." Or perhaps he did what was expected—that is, to invite the synagogue teacher home to dinner after services. We know that Jesus often taught in the synagogue. His authoritative teaching and stunning miracles had given Jesus considerable notoriety,

That's a Good Question

so having Him to dinner fell right into Simon's sense of self-importance. Or maybe, like most Pharisees, Simon felt slightly threatened by Jesus and was hoping for an opportunity to catch Him in a fault, so he could discredit Jesus.

Jesus responded to the invitation and took His place at Simon's table. In the ancient Middle East, affluent people reclined at table. Instead of chairs, there would be bench or couch-type seating. Being in a warm climate, homes were much more open. A dinner party would even spill out into an open courtyard. Dinner in Asian countries generally takes place in mid to late evening.

In the dusk shadows of approaching night, a woman snuck into the party and approached Jesus, whom she'd learned would be present. Then began a most extraordinary display of love. Weeping, she kissed and caressed Jesus' feet, washing them with her tears mixed with an expensive perfume (one of the perks of her profession), and wiping them with her long hair.

Simon noticed. Simon was offended. This was an outrage. He recognized this woman. He despised her. Muttering under his breath, he reasoned that if Jesus were truly a prophet, He would know what kind of woman was touching Him. Disgusting! Either Jesus was not a prophet at all, or He knew all about this woman and didn't care. Scandalous!

Oh, Simon, you are exposing yourself. The only people who are outraged are people who consider themselves morally superior. Outrage always says, "I wouldn't do that" or "I am better than that!"

Of course Jesus *was* a prophet, the greatest and final prophet. He was the ultimate prophet, the Son of God—very God of very God. He knew the woman very well, and he knew Simon. He knew exactly what Simon was thinking. He got Simon's attention and posed a circumstantial enquiry. "A certain moneylender had two debtors. One owed five hundred denarii [a denarius was worth a day's wage for a laborer], and the other fifty. When they could not pay, he canceled the debt of both. Now which of them will love him more?" (Luke 7:41, 42).

Simon admitted the answer—"The one. . .for whom he canceled the larger debt," and Jesus told him he had judged rightly. And then came the *real* question:

"Do you see this woman?"

One might have expected Jesus to ignore such a sinful woman. Wouldn't the pure, sinless Son of God stand against her? Wasn't He ashamed of her attentions? Why would He call for Simon to focus on *her*?

Because *she* was the debtor for whom the large debt was canceled.

And then, in a series of contrasts, Jesus nailed Simon to his smug, superior attitude.

> You gave me no water for my feet, but she wet my feet with her tears and wiped them with her hair. You gave me no kiss, but she has not ceased to kiss my feet. You did not anoint my head with oil, but she anointed my feet with precious ointment.
> (Luke 7:44–46)

With a mighty conclusion, Jesus said, "Therefore I tell you, her sins, which are many, are forgiven—for she loved much. But he who is forgiven little, loves little" (Luke 7:47). Clearly the "he who is forgiven little" refers to Simon.

Jesus admitted that the woman's sins were many. But were Simon's really fewer? Were his sins of pride, self-righteousness, superiority, self-absorption, and legalism less offensive to God than the woman's moral failures?

Sins like pride, self-righteousness, and contempt for others are, unfortunately, socially acceptable sins; unlike sexual immorality, drug abuse, alcoholism, or theft, to cite only a few examples of "disreputable" sins.

"Do you see this woman?"

The greatest contrast between these two people who crossed paths at a dinner party was not the quantity or quality of their sins. The deepest dissimilarity between them was her wholehearted love for Jesus and Simon's benevolent neglect of Him. The woman knew she was a sinner in need of rescue and therefore loved the Savior.

Simon didn't consider himself a sinner, didn't need a Savior, and therefore had slight regard for this strange man, Jesus, who claimed to be the God in the flesh, the promised Messiah. Interesting.

I am reminded of a story Jesus told, similar to the one He told Simon about the two debtors.

> Two men went up into the temple to pray, one a Pharisee and the other a tax collector. The Pharisee, standing by himself prayed thus: "I thank you that I am not like other men, extortioners, unjust, adulterers, or even like this tax collector. I fast twice a week; I give tithes of all that I get." But the tax collector, standing far off, would not even lift his eyes up to heaven, but beat his breast saying, "God, be merciful to me, a sinner." I tell you this man went down to his house justified, rather than the other. For everyone who exalts himself will be humbled, but the one who humbles himself will be exalted.
> (Luke 18:10–14)

"Do you see this woman?"

Jesus asked this question of Simon, drawing his attention to a woman Jesus knew he despised, not for the purpose of having a theological discussion about sin and forgiveness. Jesus *loved* Simon. Jesus wasn't a lover of dinner parties. He was a lover of sinners! He was accused of being a winebibber because He went to places where sinners could be found.

His question, the story of the two debtors, and His comparison of the woman and Simon in terms of their love for the Forgiver, were designed to humble Simon and bring him to understand that his need of a Savior was no less than the woman's.

"Do you see this woman?"

The feast at Simon's house ends with the most beautiful words in any language in the world: "And He said to her, 'Your sins are forgiven. Your faith has saved you; go in peace.'" Can you imagine the woman disappearing into the darkness of a Jerusalem night with a light heart, now weeping not over her sin, but over the love and forgiveness of her Savior?

"Do you see this woman?"

I was the Pharisee. Raised in a conservative Christian family, taught Bible norms from early childhood, I was a "good" girl. I fell quite naturally into legalism—that is, I was good at keeping rules. I looked good on the outside. But my heart was dark with pride, self-righteousness, superiority, and smugness, which masked fear and anger. I hurt so many people.

One night a person near and dear to me finally told me off. I will always be thankful for that. But it hurt. I smarted from it for many days. And then the gracious words from an old hymn flooded my mind: *"Nothing in my hands I bring, simply to Your cross I cling."* I loved and hated those words. I didn't want to go to God empty. Didn't I have many gifts and accomplishments to give Him? The answer came back so clearly. There is no other way to approach God except with empty hands. Forgiveness has nothing to do with what I have accomplished. It is the life and death of Jesus alone which is my only hope. Finally the fight went out of me and I experienced the sweet love and forgiveness of my Lord.

Jesus went to the dinner party to rescue Simon, and I think, being the sovereign Lord, that He did.

"Do you see this woman?"

❖

For Further Thought

Matthew 5:2–19
Matthew 5:20
Mark 7:1–8
James 4:6–10

❖

14

"Who was it that touched me?"

LUKE 8:45

And Jesus said, "Who was it that touched me?" When all denied it, Peter said, "Master, the crowds surround you and are pressing in on you!"

Jesus was on a mission. He was walking briskly with Jairus, a ruler of the synagogue, heading toward his home. Time was of the essence because Jairus' daughter was critically ill. Unlike most rulers of synagogues, who resented Jesus and tried to discredit Him, Jairus sought Jesus out, fell at His feet, and implored Him to accompany him home and rescue his daughter. Jairus believed that Jesus could work miracles.

Wherever Jesus went, crowds followed Him. Or, as in this case, they anticipated His movements and were waiting for Him when He returned from the Gerasenes. The crowd was large and insistent, and as He and His disciples walked with Jairus, they were pressed by people on every side.

Suddenly Jesus stopped cold. "Who was it that touched me?" Are you kidding? Peter pointed out the obvious: "Master, the crowds surround you and are pressing in on you" (Luke 8:45). How could you expect to single out one person who touched you? And, as if to confirm that opinion, no one in the crowd admitted touching Jesus.

Jesus persisted. "Someone touched me." Notice the singular pronoun—"someone." The crowd did not have Jesus' attention. Even Jairus had lost Jesus' attention at this point. One person alone had His attention.

". . .power has gone out from me." Jesus was aware that someone had been healed.

"Who was it that touched me?"

Who? A woman. A poor woman. A poor, sick woman. A poor, sick, desperate woman.

She had quite a story. She had once been young, healthy, vibrant, and happy. But twelve years ago, something went terribly wrong. She began to hemorrhage. After many weeks passed, she knew that it was not her normal monthly bleeding. It was scary. What was wrong with her? Not only was the physical aspect troubling, but her bleeding made her ceremonially unclean according to God's law. Being ceremonially unclean meant that she could not participate in temple worship. It also meant that she could not be touched by friends or family. She was isolated, marginalized, discounted, and bereaved. She had lost friendship, fellowship, and companionship because of her condition. Her loneliness was poignant.

Surely there were doctors who could diagnose her problem and successfully treat her. The first doctor she visited shook his head. Her condition could not be treated. Well, maybe she should get a second opinion. And a third. And a fourth. And a fifth. Soon she had spent all her income and all her savings on physicians—to no use. She had almost come to accept her impossible situation. Almost...

One day, she heard about a man named Jesus. It was rumored that He had healing powers. She began to hear testimonials from people who had been healed by Him. Who *was* He? There was no end of quasi-religious wanderers in Palestine. *But Jesus was different.* There were many ideas floating around on the subject. He claimed to be the Son of God, the promised Messiah. Could it be? Oh, she longed for it to be true. She loved God and prayed for the Messiah.

One day she joined a crowd following Jesus. It was a risky move, her being "unclean" and all. There were so many people. How would she ever get close to Him? Did she even want to get close to Him? She was just an ordinary woman. Her poor health had left her physically weak and haggard. Her condition was very private, even a little embarrassing. Her pursuit of doctors had left her in poverty. She was definitely a "nobody." She couldn't, *shouldn't* bother the great teacher. She should remain anonymous. Anyway, it looked like He was in a hurry to be somewhere else. Maybe she could just get close enough to touch His garment. If He were who He claimed to be (and she wanted so much for it to be so), He could heal her without her being noticed. It was worth a try!

"Who was it that touched me?"

Why did He have to know? Why did He want to identify her? Why did Jesus have to expose her furtive action? She wanted just to get out of there and hurry home. She had been healed. Wasn't that enough?

Deep in her heart she knew it wasn't enough. She yearned to know Jesus personally. His lovingkindness had touched her. She would be so honored to meet Him. It would surely be worth the loss of privacy.

Why did Jesus have to ask who touched Him? Because God is love. Jesus is the omniscient God. He well knew who had touched Him. He indicated that He knew she had been healed—"Power has gone out of me. . ." But He wanted the personal interaction with her. God is not a divine vending machine that dispenses good things when the right conditions are met. Prayer is not a mechanical transaction that automatically takes place when the petitioner is or does what is acceptable.

"Who was it that touched me?"

God is all about the individual. God does not deal with people as groups. He touches one person at a time. John 3:16, perhaps the most well-known verse in the Bible, says, "God so loved the world that He gave His only Son, that *whoever* believes in Him should not perish. . ." He loves the world, and saves individuals. Mark 16:15,16 records what is known as the Great Commission. It says, "Go into all the world and proclaim the gospel to the whole creation. *Whoever* believes and is baptized will be saved. . ." From the whole creation, God focuses on the single person who believes.

Throughout Scripture, we see God reaching out to His loved ones in very personal ways. Remember the three Hebrew young men in the furnace in Babylon? God didn't just deliver them from afar. He *stood with them* in the midst of the fire. There are so many images in Scripture that illustrate God's personal regard for His people—a Shepherd carrying lambs in His bosom and gently leading those who are pregnant with young (Isaiah 40:11). . .

young chicks taking shelter under the wings of the mother bird (Psalm 91:4)...a father having compassion on his children (Psalm 103:13).

When Jesus was on earth, He *touched* those who needed His help. He touched the leper (the untouchable), He touched the eyes of the blind man, He took the young daughter of Jairus *by the hand* as He raised her from her deathbed and gave her new life. He took children up on His lap and blessed them.

Jesus *could not* go on His way with Jairus and let this precious woman just melt back into the crowd. He loved her. He wanted to talk with her, to reassure her, to see her happy and healthy.

There was another reason why Jesus could not let her go unnoticed. Remember, her bleeding condition had caused her social harm. She had been ceremonially unclean for twelve years. Even her closest family and friends had to avoid her. Even the worship of God in the temple, and especially on holy days, was prohibited to her. Now that she was healed, how would she go about proving to her community that she was no longer unclean? Jesus, with His very thoughtful love, made sure that everyone knew she had been healed. He had to declare it publicly.

"Who was it that touched me?"

"When the woman saw that she was not hidden. . ." It had become hopeless to think that she could remain anonymous, quickly making it through the crowd and on her way before people were the wiser. Trembling, and falling down before Him, she had the courage, born out of the love of Jesus, to admit openly in the presence of all who could hear her why she had touched Him, and how she had been immediately healed.

Why was she trembling? One can imagine the mix of emotions that she was experiencing. Nervousness at being the object of attention before such a large crowd, surprise and awe at what had just happened to her (after twelve years of suffering), apprehension concerning what Jesus might say and do, a deep sense of unworthiness, but, most of all, enormous thanksgiving and adoration for Jesus, who had given her such an amazing gift of love.

"*And he said to her, 'Daughter, your faith has made you well. . .'*" Again, the stunningly beautiful consideration of God. Jesus referred to her faith as the agent of her healing! He didn't boast of His own power to heal. Instead, He commended her for her faith, little though it might have been.

"*Go in peace.*" There are no words to describe the relief of this little sentence. People everywhere in every generation have struggled with the conflicts, internal and external, of daily life. Daily we are buffeted by the troubles of life in a broken world. The book of Romans in chapter 8, puts it this way: that we "groan" waiting for the final redemption. We long for peace.

"*Go in peace.*" Isaiah 26:3 and 4 says of God, "You will keep him in perfect peace whose mind is stayed on you because he trusts in you." God gives this wonderful gift of peace. He wants us to live in peace. The evening news will not give any peace. God will, when we choose to trust Him.

Imagine the relief this woman felt when her twelve-year-long burden was lifted. What peace she must have known for the first time in a very long time.

And, then, just like that, Jesus went on with Jairus, Peter, John, and James to attend to a little girl who had died while Jesus conversed with the woman. Not to worry, Jesus can raise the dead! And He did.

"*Who was it that touched me?*"

❖

For Further Thought

Psalm 36:5
Isaiah 41:10
Isaiah 43:1–3
Zephaniah 3:17

❖

15

"Why are you discussing the fact that you have no bread?"

MARK 8:15

And he cautioned them, saying, "Watch out; beware of the leaven of the Pharisees and the leaven of Herod."

It's not about bread.

The Pharisees had confronted Jesus—again—asking for a miraculous sign *proving* that He was the Son of God, the promised Messiah. That recent exchange still on His mind, Jesus said to His disciples, "Watch out; beware of the leaven of the Pharisees and the leaven of Herod" (Mark 8:15).

Oops! At the word "leaven," the disciples looked at one another. They had completely forgotten to bring bread, and Jesus knew it. They were in a boat crossing the Sea of Galilee. Where were they going to get bread? They had messed up. Aware of their discomfort about bread, Jesus said,

"Why are you discussing the fact that you have no bread?"

It's not about bread. *Leaven*, when connected to the Pharisees, was a figure of speech for the *heart* and *soul* of the Pharisees' teaching and living. Leaven is a rising agent that fills the dough and enlarges it. So also, the teaching of the Pharisees, unchecked, will become a pervasive influence wherever it prevails. *"Watch out; beware. . ."* These are words of warning. There is danger about. Be careful. There is something perilous afoot.

Luke 12:1 records these words of Jesus, "Beware of the leaven of the Pharisees, which is hypocrisy." Hypocrisy is insincerity. It is pretending to be something that one is not. It is being one thing in public, and another in private.

It's not about bread. It's about the *heart*.

This goes immediately to the issue of the Pharisees repeatedly asking for a sign from Jesus to prove His divinity. They pretended to sincerely want to know Jesus, but, really, they wanted to disparage Him. Ultimately, they wanted to kill Him, and they eventually did. If they had really wanted to know Jesus' identity, they had all the Old Testament prophecies which Jesus had fulfilled perfectly. They had multiple miracles of healing, provision, even resurrection! They had Jesus' authoritative teaching, unlike anything anyone had ever heard.

Jesus used two powerful metaphors to describe the Pharisees' hypocrisy—washing a cup on the outside and leaving the inside dirty, and whitewashing a tomb and leaving it full of dead men's bones (see Matthew 23:25–28). They were the cup. They were the tomb. They were scrupulous in their attention to public virtue, while they were blithely unconcerned about purity of heart. It was for their hearing that Jesus condemned lust as equivalent to adultery, and anger as equivalent to murder. The heart matters.

> *"Why are you discussing the fact that you have no bread?"*

It's not about bread. It's about the heart. Hypocrisy exposes a disease of the soul. The disciples were focused on the wrong thing. There is the body, and there is the soul. There is the physical and there is the spiritual. There is the visible and there is the invisible. There is earth and there is heaven.

Where was their focus? Where were their hearts? Jesus said, *"Where your treasure is, there your heart will be also"* (Matthew 6:21). A large proportion of people are focused on "bread"; that is, they spend life pursuing material things, things that satisfy the body— food, shelter, clothing, health. In modern, affluent America, that can mean rich, even exotic, food, bigger and better houses (have you watched HGTV lately?), and body-conscious fitness. At the same time, little thought and even less effort is given to the condition of the heart. Spiritual pursuits are less important, if important at all.

Don't concentrate on bread. Concentrate on the more important issues of the heart. It's not okay to be publicly virtuous like the Pharisees, while tolerating impurity in the heart. Jesus addressed this very polarity exhaustively in His Sermon on the Mount, as recorded in Matthew 5–7. Consider these words:

> I tell you, do not be anxious about your life, what you will eat or what you will drink, nor about your body, what you

"Why are you discussing the fact that you have no bread?"

will put on. Is not life more than food, and the body more than clothing? Look at the birds of the air; they neither sow nor reap nor gather into barns, and yet your heavenly Father feeds them. Are you not of more value than they?

And why are you anxious about clothing? Consider the lilies of the field, how they grow: they neither toil nor spin, yet I tell you, even Solomon in all his glory was not arrayed like one of these. But if God so clothes the grass of the field, which today is alive and tomorrow is thrown into the oven, will he not much more clothe you...

Do not be anxious, saying, "What shall we eat? Or What shall we drink? Or what shall we wear?" . . .your heavenly Father knows that you need them all.
(Matthew 6:25–32)

The bottom line is this, in verse 33: "But seek first the kingdom of God and his righteousness, and all these things will be added to you."

It's not about bread. It's about priorities. The Pharisees had it all wrong, and the disciples didn't understand Jesus' warning. It's about what is important. The choice is to focus on bread or to focus on God's kingdom, which is within you—His rule of your heart.

The disciples should have understood. Jesus highlighted this fact as He continued to question them: "Do you not yet perceive or understand? Are your hearts hardened? Having eyes do you not see, and having ears do you not hear?"

Disciples, do you remember how God sent Joseph to Egypt to save that country as well as surrounding countries, including his own family from famine? Do you remember how God sent ravens to feed Elijah during a famine? Do you remember the flour and oil miraculously unfailing until the drought was over?

"Why are you discussing the fact that you have no bread?"

". . .and all these things will be added to you." It's not only that you should not focus your life's energy on external, physical, material provisions. It's that *you don't need* to be consumed with those pursuits, for "...your heavenly Father knows that you need them all" (Matthew 6:32).

Jesus taught His disciples to pray, and in the prayer He gave them, known as the Lord's Prayer, we pray "Give us this day our daily bread" (Matthew 6:11), clearly a call to trust God for the needs of our bodies.

While still in the boat with not enough bread, Jesus zeroed in on this as He continued to talk to His slow-to-understand disciples:

> "And do you not remember? When I broke the five loaves for the five thousand, how many baskets full of broken pieces did you take up?" They said to him, "Twelve." "And the seven for the four thousand, how many baskets full of broken pieces did you take up?" And they said to him, "Seven." And he said to them, "Do you not yet understand?"
> (Mark 8:18b–21)

It's not about bread. It's about the heart. Guard your heart. Stay away from the hypocrisy of the Pharisees.

Not that many years hence, the early church would struggle with the hypocrisy of legalism as argued by the Judaizers. Jesus' warning was so important.

Guard your heart. Make that your priority. Make that your focus. Seek, above all else, the kingdom of God, His gracious rule. Trust God to take care of the "bread." He knows what you need. He notes when a sparrow falls. You are so much more valuable than sparrows. The very hairs of your head are numbered! Imagine it!

> Now to him who is able to do far more abundantly than all that we ask or think, according to the power at work within us, to him be glory in the church and in Christ Jesus throughout all generations, forever and ever. Amen.
> (Ephesians 3:20, 21)

"Why are you discussing the fact that you have no bread?"

❖

"Why are you discussing the fact that you have no bread?"

For Further Thought

Psalm 23:1,5

Matthew 4:1–4

Matthew 6:11

Philippians 4:19

1 Timothy 6:6–10

❖

16

"Why are you so afraid?"

MARK 4:40

He said to them, "Why are you so afraid? Have you still no faith?"

Many of Jesus' disciples were former fisherman, so a fishing boat was often available to Him. His ministry caused Him and the disciples to crisscross the Sea of Galilee.

On this occasion, it was evening when Jesus suggested that they go by boat to the other side of the Sea. "And a great windstorm arose. . ." *Great* is the operative word here. This storm was severe.

These former fishermen had fished the Sea of Galilee for decades. They were skilled sailors. They knew how to handle a fishing boat, and they knew every inch of the Sea of Galilee. They had also, over the span of their fishing careers, experienced many storms. It seems that the topography of the area, combined with the climate, spawned sudden, frequent storms on the Sea of Galilee. They had a lot of practice navigating storms, even ferocious ones, and they could handle their craft. On water, they were capable.

And then something hit them that they couldn't manage. This storm was of a different quality. It happened so fast. Almost before they could react, the waves were beating the boat almost to pieces, and the boat was being swamped. Knee-deep in water, they tried every defense in a sailor's playbook, but the storm was clearly winning.

In a broken world, damaged by the fall, we have come to expect difficulties. As with the disciples, we can manage most of life's challenges, even storms. We are pretty self-sufficient, independent, and capable. We even pride ourselves at times that we can cope with what life throws at us. We also have support systems that have our backs. In a pinch, we can call on family, friends, clergy, doctors, counselors, and other experts. For a rainy day, we rely on our jobs, our savings, our possessions.

Then something comes along we can't handle. Our support system fails us. Our rainy-day preparations are no comfort. We freak out. Suddenly we see ourselves as weak, incompetent, unable. Hope fades. Panic makes the pit of our stomachs ache. We are the disciples in a fishing boat in the mother of all storms.

There was someone asleep in the bottom of the boat. While the disciples were panicked, frantic, a mass of frenetic activity, someone was at peace. Who?

None other than the Lord God Almighty, the Lord of the heavenly armies, the Promised Messiah, Lamb of God. He, King of kings and Lord of lords, the Sovereign Master of everything, the Alpha and Omega, the Good Shepherd, the Light and Salvation, the Refuge and Strength, the High Tower that one runs into for safety, was napping in the boat!

He walked on water, fed 5,000 with a few loaves and fish, raised Jairus' daughter and Lazarus from the dead, healed countless invalids of every kind, turned water into wine, and preached like no one anyone had ever heard.

That One was sleeping through the storm.

The disciples finally awakened Jesus, and, as they did so, demonstrated their unbelief. Instead of humbly confessing their previous self-sufficiency and independence, and instead of humbly admitting their inability in the face of the storm and asking Him for His help, *they accused Him!*

What? Yes, they accused Him with these words, "Teacher, do you not care that we are perishing?" This is the bottom line. It is the point of their unbelief. They didn't question His ability. They questioned His *desire*. They had some faith in His power, but they had no faith in His love for them. His nap in the boat was misinterpreted as lack of caring.

Before one feels superior to the hapless disciples, one must reflect upon the fact that *accusing* God is a common response to suffering. We take His blessing every day, but when something goes badly wrong, the first question we whisper in anguish is "Why?" We, too, are pretty sure of God's power, but does He love us? He could have changed the circumstances, but He didn't. Does He know how hurt we are? Does He understand the devastation? Is this love?

"Why are you so afraid?"

"Why are you so afraid?"

Jesus asked this significant question. Why, indeed. The storm was so furious that it had overwhelmed the disciples' sense of perspective. It had completely taken over their field of vision. It had blinded them to everything else, including the One sleeping in close proximity to their frenzied activity.

It also had become pervasive in their thinking. It had taken their total attention. Their minds had been consumed with their fear. They had lost faith.

"Why are you so afraid?"

This question was immediately followed by another question of Jesus. *"Have you still no faith?"* "Still"—Jesus asks if, after all the time they had spent with Him, after all they had seen and heard, they had persisted in a large degree of unbelief.

Faith is the answer to fear. It is the only adequate answer to fear.

The important thing about faith is the object of faith. Sometimes we hear talk about "people of faith." Or we hear the superficial suggestion, "Have faith." *Faith in what?* People place "faith" in all kinds of things—other people, possessions, security schemes, their experience or education, medicine, insurance policies, and bank accounts.

Only one object of faith is worthy—God in three Persons, the blessed Holy Trinity. In this situation, as is always the case, the disciples' faith in *everything else* failed them, just as our faith in *everything else* always fails us.

Does God really care? The Bible is full of examples of the awesome power of God. If one traces those displays of authority and might, one will conclude that God always uses His great power *for the benefit of His people.* When Jesus walked this earth, He consistently refused to use His power to benefit Himself, but He used it freely to rescue needy sinners. He never sought fame, even though His stunning supernatural ability could have given it to Him.

God's power demonstrates His love. Even when His power is destructive, as when He judges His enemies, it is for the benefit of His people. God's power accomplishes what His love demands.

His power and His love are like two sides of the same coin.

Then why was He sleeping while His disciples struggled with a terrifying reality? Why do devoted followers of Jesus in every generation suffer? Why do we face storms? Why are we sometimes blindsided by emergencies we cannot handle? Why are our hopes often disappointed in crushing blows?

Could it be that the severity of the storm blinds us to the true meaning of the love of God? We doubt His regard of us because we do not understand His *purpose* in us.

"Why are you so afraid?"

> For *he* commanded and raised the stormy wind, which lifted up the waves of the sea. They mounted up to heaven; they went down to the depths; their courage melted away in their evil plight; they reeled and staggered like drunken men and were at their wits' end. Then they cried to the LORD. . .and he delivered them. . . .
> (Psalm 107:25–28)

God is the Lord of creation. He rules absolutely over all the forces of the natural world. Nothing is out of His control.

Counterintuitively, storms are an expression of God's love. Storms are not an indication that God is uncaring, as the disciples accused. Rather, they are necessary for our spiritual growth, just as strenuous exercise is necessary for our physical growth, or challenging times for our growth in character.

STORMS EXPOSE US. There is nothing like a fierce storm to reveal how soft, how spoiled we have been. They expose our trust in *idols of the heart* (like self-importance, dependence on bank accounts and insurance policies, or love of material things) that fail us when times are tough.

STORMS HUMBLE US. When the boat is filling with water, we learn quickly how weak and helpless we really are. Pride in our abilities and accomplishments looks foolish.

"Why are you so afraid?"

STORMS TEACH US. There are precious lessons about God in His awesome beauty and grace that we learn no other place than in the middle of a storm. In a storm, God gets our attention and shows us marvels of lovingkindness that we otherwise would never know.

STORMS DISCIPLINE US. When we are bebopping along and everything is sunshine and peace, we can get complacent and lazy. Spiritual disciplines like Bible study and prayer can slack off a bit or become perfunctory and therefore boring. But when there is a storm which threatens everything we hold dear, we become serious about knowing God, who is our only hope.

STORMS DEEPEN OUR FAITH. I am quite sure that the disciples never again questioned Jesus' love for them. The display of raw power used on their behalf was a tutorial in faith that they never forgot. First Peter 1:6,7 says: "In this [salvation] you rejoice, though now for a little while, if necessary, you have been grieved by various trials, so that the tested genuineness of your faith—more precious than gold that perishes, though it is tested by fire—may be found to result in praise and glory and honor at the revelation of Jesus Christ." Yes, the love of God brings storms into our lives to refine our faith.

There is a lovely old hymn by the great poet, William Cowper, that captures the meaning of faith in the middle of the storm so well.

God moves in a mysterious way
His wonders to perform;
He plants His footsteps in the sea,
and rides upon the storm.

Ye fearful saints, fresh courage take;
the clouds ye so much dread
are big with mercy and shall break
in blessings on your head.

> *Judge not the Lord by feeble sense,*
> *but trust Him for His grace;*
> *behind a frowning providence*
> *He hides a smiling face.*[5]

Jesus did care. He cared about the awful fright the disciples had from the storm. He wanted them to learn to trust Him, so that they would not be so frightened again.

They were never in any danger from the storm. He was there with them. Asleep, He was a better protection than anyone or anything else wide awake!

It was too easy really. He rebuked the wind, and said to the sea, *"Peace! Be still!"* And instantly, there was calm. The boat righted itself, and we can imagine how the disciples in unison let out a deep sigh.

And then, after a moment's reflection, they really were afraid! They were not any longer afraid of the elements. *They were looking at a man with scary power*. The glory of God was revealed to them there in that boat, and they would never be the same. "And they were filled with great fear and said to one another, 'Who is this, that even wind and sea obey him?'" Who, indeed!

I can even imagine that one or two of them, including Peter, of course, knelt down before Him, drenched in sea water, and worshiped in awe.

It is said that the only cure for the fear of earthy things is the fear of God.

> *"Why are you so afraid?"*

❖

---

[5] William Cowper, *God Moves in a Mysterious Way*

"Why are you so afraid?"

For Further Thought
....

Romans 8:31–39

Matthew 10:28

2 Timothy 1:7

1 John 4:18

❖

17

"Who do you say that I am?"

MATTHEW 16:15

He said to them, "But who do you say that I am?"

Is there a more important question? One's insight into the identity of Jesus of Nazareth is determinative of all of life and eternity. It is metaphysics boiled down to its essence. It is simply ultimate. It is the pivot point, the fulcrum of history from creation to paradise.

Jesus prefaces this question with another, more general question: "Who do people say that the Son of Man is?" Jesus most often referred to Himself as "the Son of Man," emphasizing His humanity. Philippians 2 states that when Jesus came to earth, He humbled Himself. He set aside the prerogatives of deity in order to take the place of a servant of mankind, and finally to die for the sins of the world. Jesus didn't go around claiming His divinity, although He clearly owned it when it was important to do so.

"Who do *people* say that the Son of Man is?" People. . . One constant feature of Jesus' ministry was the presence of a crowd. Wherever He went, masses of people followed Him. The Gospels seem to show three distinct elements in the crowd. I like to call them the *rubbernecks,* the *professionals,* and the *beggars.*

The rubbernecks were the curiosity seekers, the thrill seekers. They had heard rumors of Jesus' astounding miracles and they wanted to see some. They were voyeurs who liked the excitement of seeing and hearing something new.

The professionals were the religious leaders—Scribes, Pharisees, Sadducees, Temple Rulers, Rabbis. They followed Jesus around looking for an opportunity to prove Him wrong. They were the religious intelligentsia, proud of their knowledge of Old Testament law, but Jesus often contradicted their teaching. Their little kingdom of ecclesiastical power was threatened by Jesus. He called them out for their hypocrisy. They were desperate to find a reason to end His influence.

But the beggars! They were simple folk searching for grace.

They were unashamed to confess that they had needs and believed that Jesus could meet those needs. They just wanted to get near enough to Him to get His attention. They could see His compassion and believed that He would have mercy upon them—if they could only get close enough.

I want to be a beggar. I am afraid that I, like the professionals, have often trusted in my own wisdom or piety. I'm afraid that I, like the rubbernecks, have at times read the Bible to satisfy my curiosity rather than to know God. But I know more every day that I need Him. I want to be a lifelong seeker after God Himself, and the rescue of His grace that I deeply need.

Jesus' identity was the question that swirled around Him from the moment He came on the scene until the day He ascended into heaven. Even as He hung on the cross, His identity was challenged. King Herod had a sign posted on the cross, designating Jesus as "The King of the Jews." The Pharisees strenuously objected, but Herod persisted.

The disciples answered that general question, "Who do people say that I am?" They reflected that some said that Jesus was John the Baptist, and some rumored that He was Elijah or Jeremiah or another of the prophets. These "people" were the curious and the needy. The professionals liked to call Him a glutton and a drunkard, a friend of sinners—even the servant of Beelzebub! But the large group of rubbernecks and beggars—they thought that perhaps one of the dead prophets had come to life in the body of Jesus of Nazareth. Everyone had an opinion. To gossip about who He could possibly be was something of a pastime. There was no disrespect intended in their ideas about who Jesus was, but they missed the mark by a mile! If they only knew His true identity!

And then the *real* question. Jesus got direct, specific and personal.

"Who do you say that I am?"

This is the *only* question. What others may or may not think is just an abstraction.

Jesus posed the only question that matters. "What do *you* think? God is always personal. His intervention in the affairs of men is always one-on-one. He doesn't rescue people in groups. He doesn't save people in general. He is the Shepherd who leaves the flock to go find the *one* sheep who had gone astray. He wants *you*.

Jesus had specifically chosen these twelve men to be with Him throughout His ministry on earth. He spent most of His time with them. He *loved* them. He came to rescue them, to give them faith and hope and eternal life. He knew that they would become the founders of the church, leaders in spreading the gospel to the whole world. He longed that they know Him. His heart yearned to know that they "got" who He was.

Peter, always ahead of the rest, outspoken, intense, proactive. . .of course Peter answered sincerely from his heart, and without hesitation, "You are the Christ, the Son of the Living God." And that is a mouthful!

Christ means *anointed one* or one set apart for a unique mission. It is synonymous with the term *Messiah*. It speaks of the "promised one," and refers to all the Old Testament prophecies of which He is the object.

It began in the Garden of Eden, after God found Adam and Eve hiding in fear because they had broken covenant with God. In His unparalleled mercy, He promised that one day the progeny of Eve would crush the head of Satan, the evil serpent. That *seed of the woman* is Christ.

The culture of the Israelites, dictated to Moses in the form of the moral and the ceremonial law, was in its entirety a revelation of the coming of Messiah. Jesus was declared to be the great and final prophet, priest, and king of His people, and the Old Testament prepared every Jew to know what that meant. Centuries of prophets, priests, and kings in Israel prepared them to know the person and work of Christ.

The great prophecy of the coming "child" in Isaiah 9—"wonderful counselor, mighty God, everlasting Father, prince of peace, the one whose government will never end"—gave hope to God's people. So, too, did the poignant picture of the suffering servant in Isaiah 53: ". . .he bore our griefs and carried our sorrows. . . he was wounded for our transgressions, crushed for our iniquities, chastised for our peace and beaten for our healing."

These are among many Old Testament promises that foretell the life, work, and atoning death of Jesus of Nazareth.

Peter's declaration of Jesus' identity encompasses all the beautiful, stunningly glorious descriptions of Him presented in Scripture: Jesus of Nazareth, the Messiah, is the hope of the ages, the desire of nations, the light of the world, the lamb of God, the personification of God's grace for sinners, the blessed Redeemer, the pearl of great price, the treasure of surpassing value, the One possessing all authority and power in heaven and earth, the rose of Sharon, the bright and morning star, the only savior.

". . .the Son of the Living God." The Nicene Creed cannot be improved in its statement that He was "born of the Father before all ages, God of God, Light of Light, very God of very God, begotten, not made, of one substance with the Father, by whom all things were made. . ." This is the meaning of Peter's confession!

". . .living God." God is not an idea. He is not a force. He is a near and present Person, alive and active in the affairs of men. He makes the sun rise every morning, sends the rain on the just and the unjust, rules over the nations, and actively draws sinners to repentance and faith.

The creed reflects Peter's answer, not the other way around. Peter's words were not primarily a statement of theology. They were not first of all a statement of doctrine. They were *an expression of worship.*

In confessing his understanding of the true nature of Jesus of Nazareth, Peter was:

- A sinner who could never rescue himself in the presence of his Savior
- A debtor in the presence of his Redeemer
- A creature in the presence of his Creator
- A finite, dependent man in the presence of Sovereignty
- An unlearned fisherman in the presence of Omniscience
- An alien in the presence of the Lover of his soul

The answer of Peter was an act of adoration. He was not just in the presence of greatness. He was in the presence of the ultimate. And the ultimate was not a transcendent royal, intimidating in His glory, but One who gave up everything to draw near to sinners, and to give His life for their rescue. *Hallelujah, what a Savior!*

Jesus affirmed Peter's answer with these words: "Blessed are you, Simon Bar-Jonah. For flesh and blood has not revealed this to you, but my Father who is in heaven" (Matthew 16:17). Peter's faith in Jesus of Nazareth as the promised Messiah, the Son of God in the flesh, was not the product of his intellect. It was not his superior perception or his astute observation. This faith is a gift of God. The beginning of faith is a revelation of Christ. The first hint of a sinner coming home is God's opening of his eyes to the supreme value of Jesus Christ. God Himself must reveal to the sinner the treasure that is the person and work of Jesus of Nazareth. Flesh and blood—that is, human beings—cannot reveal this.

"Who do you say that I am?"

❖

For Further Thought

Isaiah 9:2–7

Romans 10:9–11

Colossians 1:15–19

Philippians 2:9–11

❖

18

"Do you want to go away as well?"

JOHN 6:67

So Jesus said to the twelve, "Do you want to go away as well?"

They had been following Jesus for several weeks, maybe longer. There was quite a large group of regular folk like themselves who hung around wherever He went. Of course, they had to break away now and then to attend to their work, but as much as possible they traveled along, but at a bit of a distance, so as not to be singled out by Him as others had been. However, when He seemed to be doing something supernatural, their curiosity got the best of them and they crowded in closer so they could see.

He was a fascinating figure. They just couldn't stay away. Who was He? Some people said that His home was Nazareth and that He came from a large family. Everyone gossiped about His life. It was told that He apprenticed as a carpenter—seemed to be a family business—but *this* man was unlike any carpenter they had ever known. He spoke like some kind of religious teacher. He often referred to the Old Testament Scriptures—like He really knew them well. It didn't add up. It was well known that Palestine had more than its share of religious gurus wandering around claiming this and that, sometimes scamming people out of their little money.

This man was different. His teaching was like nothing they had ever heard! It was spellbinding. It wasn't "high and mighty" like many synagogue lectures, yet in a quiet way it came with authority. It had the ring of truth, and sometimes their hearts filled with hope as they listened to Him.

And His miracles! They were not magic tricks, for sure. The blind man who was healed was well known in the community. They knew him before, and they knew him after. His healing was for real, and his life was changed just as were so many others.

One amazing day, they found themselves sitting on a hillside amid a huge gathering, listening in astonishment to Jesus' teaching. They were so rapt that they were careless of the passage of time. Even little children seemed captivated, uncharacteristically quiet. Before anyone realized it, the day had waned, and Jesus' discourse came to a close. Suddenly their awareness of hunger became acute. Was it possible that they hadn't eaten all day? They hadn't thought to bring food, and they dreaded the long trek home before they could eat. How would the children fare?

As the crowd began to gather up their families to head home, a young lad near them rose, clutching a small lunch container. They watched, curious, as he made his way forward and handed Jesus his lunch. Why? Surely this child was also hungry. What would Jesus do? They watched, transfixed, as Jesus lifted the lunch heavenward and gave thanks. The rest was the stuff of legend, although, in this case, it was certainly real. They would one day tell their grandchildren how this huge crowd of people were fed by the disciples passing out the boy's lunch, piece by piece. At first, they took only a little, not sure there would be enough for everyone. But miraculously, there was plenty for all to eat until they were satisfied. They even watched, in wonder, as the twelve disciples found twelve baskets in which to place the *leftovers!*

News of this miracle of food traveled quickly, and the next day an enlarged crowd was eager to find Jesus. Only when they did, He had some hard words for them. Knowing their hearts, He confronted them with their motive for seeking Him out: ". . .you are seeking me, not because you saw signs, but because you ate your fill of the loaves. Do not labor for the food that perishes, but for the food that endures to eternal life which the Son of Man will give to you" (John 6:26,27). He knew what they were thinking. Imagine never again having to concern oneself with providing food. Imagine a Messiah who could and would feed enormous crowds anytime they were hungry!

Did they hear what He said? He contrasted food that perishes (regular food) with food that endures to eternal life. Further, He promised to give them the latter.

The discussion continued, and the people actually asked Jesus for a sign that would convince them to believe in Him. Were they serious? Really? Just the day before, Jesus fed them with a small boy's small lunch, and now they needed *another* sign? Truly? It seems that when one has a heart of unbelief, no number of miracles with ever be enough.

Then Jesus shocked them to their core. As they sought to continue the conversation about bread by bringing up the manna which their forefathers ate in the wilderness—*bread from heaven*—Jesus countered that the manna was still *bread that perishes*. It didn't last one day before spoiling. Jesus then uttered the words loved by believers and offensive to others: "I am the bread of life; whoever comes to me shall not hunger, and whoever believes in me shall never thirst" (John 6:35).

Hold on. Isn't this Jesus of Nazareth? We know His father Joseph. We know His family. How can He claim to have come down from heaven?

He repeated His assertion that He was the bread of life. Then He went even further:

> . . .unless you eat the flesh of the Son of Man and drink His blood, you have no life in you. Whoever feeds on my flesh and drinks my blood has eternal life, and I will raise him up on the last day. For my flesh is true food, and my blood is true drink.
> (John 6:53–55)

Oh, those were hard words. They offended Jesus' audience. To them, to eat human flesh was cannibalism and abhorrent. And the Old Testament law forbade the drinking of blood. From that time on, they began to withdraw from Him.

Sadly, they didn't understand. They were simply too fixated on physical, material things. They thought they understood *bread*. Bread is a universal staple throughout the world. Every country, every culture and language has its form of bread. *Bread* is often used as a metaphor for everything needful for physical life, health, and well-being. That is what they knew. That is where they lived. These ordinary people spent the days of their lives working for *bread*. Some of them even prayed for bread.

They didn't understand that Jesus was not speaking literally when He spoke of eating His flesh and drinking His blood. He was speaking a spiritual truth. Eating a meal is a picture of feeding on Christ. Receiving Jesus into our hearts by His Holy Spirit is similar to taking food into our stomachs, and just as a person will die without food, so a person will die spiritually without Jesus Christ—for unless you eat the flesh of the Son of Man and drink His blood, you have *no life* in you.

What they missed was that physical bread can never fill the emptiness, the hunger, of the soul. No amount of material "stuff" can ever satisfy the hunger of one's heart. To try to satisfy the emptiness inside with physical, material things is an exercise in futility, and therefore frustration. God alone can fill the heart. He promises to indwell by His Holy Spirit the heart of anyone who turns from his own way and believes the gospel, embracing the perfect work and redeeming death of Jesus of Nazareth. And the fruit of the Holy Spirit inside one's heart is love, joy, peace, patience, kindness, goodness, faithfulness, gentleness, and self-control (see Galatians 5).

They still wanted the bread—the physical, material kind. And they still foolishly thought that having "enough" material provisions would make them happy. For a while the excitement they felt following Jesus and seeing His miracles awed them enough to mask the hunger of their souls. But when it came right down to it, they couldn't believe this stuff about eating flesh and drinking blood, and they couldn't believe that the son of Joseph, the carpenter, came down from heaven. Oh well, another day, another imposter, another disappointment.

And so, after this, many of His followers turned back and no longer walked with Him. So, Jesus turned to the twelve disciples and said,

> *"Do you want to go away as well?"*

Again, Simon Peter answered. He appeared to be the spokesman for the group. He answered the question with another question, "To whom shall we go?" Go where? Pursue what?

I can imagine Peter's mind turning. Go away? Where else, what else, who else could ever satisfy our hearts the way this simple carpenter, the Messiah, Son of the Living God has? Go back to fishing? Go back to the teaching of the Pharisees and Scribes? Go back to our little, mundane lives of longing, trying to make sense of it all?

Then, remonstrating, Peter added a gigantic NO with a definitive verdict: "YOU HAVE THE WORDS OF ETERNAL LIFE." You *only* have the words of eternal life.

Eternal life does not designate life after death only. Eternal life is a *quality* of life here and now. The believer has eternity in his heart. All the rough and tumble of life in a broken world is transformed by the supernatural within—that is, by God's grace administered by the indwelling Holy Spirit. The believer has the "big sky" perspective. He views all of life from the vantage point of eternity. And it *satisfies* his soul. It *satisfies*, despite the struggles, disappointments, and griefs of life here and now.

This quality of life—everlasting life—is found only in Jesus of Nazareth, the "Holy One of God," as Peter goes on to describe Him.

"Do you want to go away as well?" "To whom shall we go? You have the words of eternal life."

The disciples know absolutely that nothing and no one else would ever be enough. All the "bread" in the world would leave them craving for more. To go anyplace else was simply unthinkable. Eternity had captured their souls in the person of Jesus Christ.

The disciples, with the exception of Judas, would stay.

The crowd left.

"Do you want to go away as well?"

❖

For Further Thought

Psalm 42:1
Isaiah 55:1–13
John 7:37,38
Colossians 1:15–20

❖

19

"Where are the nine?"

LUKE 17:17

Then Jesus answered, "Were not ten cleansed? Where are the nine?"

"And as [Jesus] entered a village, He was met by ten lepers." There are no coincidental meetings with God. Jesus was where He was, when He was, in order to meet ten lepers. This meeting was planned in eternity. Jesus loved ten lepers and wanted to heal them.

He was on His way to Jerusalem, where the most significant events of His life and ministry would soon occur. He was in a kind of no man's land, on the border between Galilee and Samaria. The Samaritans were half Jewish, and, as mixed breeds, they were considered by Jews to be undesirables.

It is noteworthy that Jesus singled out Samaritans in a positive way during His ministry. Remember the story Jesus told about the "good Samaritan," who, at great expense to himself, cared for a Jewish victim of crime. Remember the Samaritan woman who gave Jesus water at her well, and in turn was given the water of eternal life. Most Jews would go a great, circuitous distance to avoid passing through Samaria, but not Jesus. More about Samaria and Samaritans later in this drama.

Leprosy is a terrible disease. Today, modern medical science has discovered effective treatments for leprosy, although there is no cure. Thought to be a skin condition, because lepers have the appearance of bumps and blotches on their skin, it is actually a disease of the nervous system. It causes damage and even death to nerve endings, resulting in loss of feeling. Lepers are disfigured because, without the sensation of pain, they wound themselves repeatedly. It is said that a leper while sleeping can have a finger completely gnawed off by a rodent and never know of it until morning when he sees his hand. Because leprosy is so hideous, and is contagious (not by touch, but by respiratory droplets in the air), lepers are strictly separated from the community.

Leviticus 13:45 and 46 describe God's law concerning lepers: "The leprous person who has the disease shall wear torn clothes and let the hair of his head hang loose, and he shall cover his upper lip and cry out, 'Unclean, unclean.' He shall remain unclean as long as he has the disease. He is unclean. He shall live alone. His dwelling shall be outside the camp." Of course, these directions were given to protect the general population from the disease, but for a leper, the necessary social isolation was a form of suffering equal to, or perhaps greater than, the physical suffering. Being forced to live apart from the community meant certain poverty, and lepers almost always became beggars in order to survive.

It is a testimony to Jesus' fame that these lepers knew His reputation. Even some outcast lepers had heard about Him. They heard that He would be in the vicinity, and approached Him, but at a distance. "Jesus, Master, have mercy on us," they cried together with a loud voice to get His attention. They cried with a loud voice in anguish and desperation.

The word *Master* in this instance designates someone who stands above, as an overseer, a supervisor, a superior.

Asking for mercy implies one's unworthiness. The lepers asked Jesus for intervention that they did not deserve. They appealed to His compassion. It is to be noticed that they did not ask Jesus to heal them. They asked for mercy. Did they want alms? Did they want some kind of material provision? They had lived in an impossible situation for so long that their expectations were small.

Equally remarkable, Jesus did not straightaway heal them. He didn't touch them. He did not pronounce them cleansed. Instead, He gave them a directive. *"Go and show yourselves to the priests."* According to Old Testament law, if an unclean person became clean—that is, recovered from his ailment—he had to go to the priests, be examined, and go through a ritual cleansing before being admitted back into society. *Going to the priests* was a clue. Could it be? Did they dare to hope?

"And as they went they were cleansed." Just imagine that scene. One leper looks down at his hand, and then his arm, and sees that all the skin irregularities are gone. His missing fingers have grown back! Could it be? Then he looks self-consciously at the leper next to him. His face is clear. His nose is the right shape again. His eyes are clear. One by one, hearts pounding, the lepers examine themselves and each other. It's unbelievable!

Notice that they were not healed until they started on the journey to the priests. This is the *obedience of faith*. It reminds me of the children of Israel at the Jordan River. There was no way that great company could cross that mighty river. God promised to part the waters just as He had parted the waters of the Red Sea when they left Egypt. But He would not part the waters until the feet of the priests entered the river. When their feet got wet, God parted the waters and the whole company walked through on dry ground. Remember the man in the synagogue with a withered arm. Jesus asked him to stretch it out, the very thing he could not do. As he nevertheless did so, his arm was instantly normal—strong and healthy. To obey *before* the miracle is received is the demonstration of faith that God commends.

"Then one of them, when he saw that he was healed, turned back praising God with a loud voice, and he fell on his face at Jesus' feet, giving Him thanks" (Luke 17:15, 16).

These no-longer-lepers suddenly had a lot to do! They could hardly wait to see the priests and begin the process of cleansing, which would take at least eight days. The sooner it was completed, the sooner they could get on with life. Imagine being able to reconnect with family! And think of this: they would be beggars no more. They would have to find work. New lodgings, new clothing. . .it was mind-boggling! Their new life was starting, and it would be very busy.

However, one former leper was not in such a hurry. His heart and mind swelled with amazement and joy. He could hardly take it all in. And he wasn't thinking about all the possibilities before him in life. He was thinking about the man from Galilee who had compassion on him. He couldn't follow the others in such haste to start a new life. He just had to turn back and *"give thanks."*

Giving thanks is not the same as feeling thankful. Throughout Scripture, we are commanded to "give thanks." Psalm 118:1 is one among many similar exhortations in the Psalms: "Oh give thanks to the LORD, for He is good; for his steadfast love endures forever!" In the New Testament, 1 Thessalonians 5:18 directs us to ". . .give thanks in all circumstances. . . ." One can have vague sentiments of gratitude and remain passive. Giving thanks requires action. It is something one *does*.

Thanksgiving is part of worship. Broadly speaking, adoration praises God for who He is. Thanksgiving praises God for what He has done, what He is doing, and what He will do.

Thanksgiving recognizes God as the Creator and Sustainer of the physical world. The sun rises at His command. Thanksgiving recognizes God as the Sovereign Controller of every situation, both cosmically and in the minute details of one's life. He is the ultimate cause, the source of everything that happens. Thanksgiving recognizes God as the Giver of every good and perfect gift.

Observe the *doing*. The one former leper:

1. TURNED BACK. That is, he turned his back on all the activities that the others were so eager to start. He went the other way. Some may have said that he went "the wrong way." The road less traveled?
2. PRAISED GOD WITH A LOUD VOICE. He saw God in Jesus. He said *words* of praise. He said them loudly, careless of others who may have been noticing. He was intense, passionate. Just as he, a few minutes earlier, had cried out for mercy, now he cried out in praise.
3. FELL ON HIS FACE AT JESUS' FEET. This was a huge expression of humility before a superior. One former leper knew that Jesus did for him what he never could have done for himself. He had been helpless and hopeless. The most he had hoped for on most days was a few crumbs of pity, maybe a few alms—enough to get him fed for one more day. Jesus changed everything. He would be forever a debtor to this humble carpenter from Galilee who was God in the flesh.

The old hymn, *When I Survey the Wondrous Cross,* says it well.

> *Were the whole realm of nature mine*
> *That were a present far too small*
> *Love so amazing, so divine*
> *Demands my soul, my life, my all.*[6]

"Where are the nine?"

The question was not "Where were they geographically?" They might even have been still visible, hurrying away down the road. The question was "Why were nine healed lepers not giving thanks as the one did?" To whom was the rhetorical question addressed—to the disciples, to the one leper, to bystanders? It was meant to provoke thoughtful reflection on the part of all those who heard it.

Nine former lepers marveled at their good fortune. No doubt, they were grateful in some indistinct way. But they were much too busy to *give thanks*. They didn't have time to turn back. Jesus was not preeminent in their thinking. They were full of themselves. Maybe they gave themselves some little credit for their transformation. After all, they were in the right place at the right time, weren't they?

They were totally distracted by all the possibilities before them. Obviously, they were going to live for all the enjoyments that had escaped them in their previous leper lives. Their hearts were in the wrong place. Colossians 3:2 speaks clearly to this situation: "Set your minds on things that are above, not on things that are on earth." The word *minds* is otherwise translated *affections*. Jesus' words recorded in Matthew 6:21 are equally relevant: "For where your treasure is, there your heart will be also." Nine former lepers demonstrated that their hearts had the exact wrong focus. The glorious, gracious, altogether lovely person who had totally changed their lives would become a nice, but distant, memory. He who had scary power had used it on their behalf because He loved them. *But they had no time!*

And then Jesus calls attention to the fact that the one former leper was a "foreigner" (Luke 17:18). Some translations read "Samaritan." Why did Jesus do this? Was it to shame the Jews who

---

6   Isaac Watts, *When I Survey the Wondrous Cross*

demeaned the Samaritans? One thing is clear. The stunning grace of God knows no national, ethnic, or racial distinctions.

And Jesus said to the one former leper still prostrate at His feet, "Rise and go your way; your faith has made you well." I am pretty sure that "well" meant not just well in body, but also well in soul. This man was not healed just to enjoy the rest of his life in this world. He was healed for eternity in another world. He was given *eternal life*. And that is a far greater cause for giving thanks than any physical blessings could ever be.

"Where are the nine?"

❖

For Further Thought

Psalm 100:1–5
Psalm 118:1,28,29
Philippians 4:4–7
1 Thessalonians 5:18

❖

20

"So, could you not watch with me one hour?"

MATTHEW 26:40

And he came to the disciples and found them sleeping. And he said to Peter, "So, could you not watch with me one hour?"

They had reached Jerusalem, Jesus and His disciples. The city was crowded because it was the feast of the Passover, one of the most important celebrations of the Jewish calendar, drawing to Jerusalem all Jews within traveling distance.

It was a stressful time. Jesus had been saying some strange things like:

". . . the Son of Man will be delivered up to be crucified. . ."

". . . she has done it [anointing His head with expensive perfume] to prepare me for burial. . ."

". . . you will all fall away because of me this night. . ."

". . . one of you will betray me. . ."

and to Peter, even more astonishing words, ". . .before the rooster crows, you will deny me three times."

What did it all mean? They didn't begin to understand all those clues, but clearly something huge and disturbing was about to happen. They were exhausted, physically and emotionally . . . apprehensive.

The Garden called Gethsemane seemed like a good place for a bit of rest and relief from the crowds. Most of the disciples were instructed to sit and wait, while Jesus took Peter and the sons of Zebedee, James and John, and retreated farther into the park.

Jesus indicated to the three that He was in great sorrow *"even to death"* and asked them to watch with Him. What does "watch" mean? Today we are familiar with a "tornado watch" or a "neighborhood watch." It implies that there is possible imminent danger. Keep alert! Be aware! Be on your guard! Keep a lookout! It implies that one should use all one's senses to detect and avoid peril.

Then Jesus went even farther into the garden, fell on His face, and prayed, "My Father, if it be possible, let this cup pass from me; nevertheless, not as I will, but as you will" (Matthew 26:39). The Gospel of Luke adds further detail, "And being in agony he prayed more earnestly; and his sweat became like great drops of blood falling down to the ground" (Luke 22:44).

When He returned to His disciples, they were sleeping.

"So, could you not watch with me one hour?"

While the disciples were sleeping, just a short distance away *the* battle of the ages was taking place. The war to end all wars was right then and there occurring on the battlefield of Jesus' heart. The unspeakable agony was so intense that even His physical body nearly exploded as He sweat large drops of blood. Jesus was being assaulted.

All of the forces of hell coalesced to persuade Jesus that He could not possibly endure the cross, that the ponderous burden of the sins of the world, coupled with the abandonment of His heavenly Father, simply would be unbearable. The fate of mankind hung in the balance. The destiny of the whole world was at stake. If evil won this fight and the Son of God capitulated to His dread, the damage would be incalculable. The result would be unthinkable. Eternal damnation would reign in the lives of everyone everywhere, all the time. Heaven would be lost.

If the disciples had realized this. . .

Jesus *did* realize all this. Yet, His response to His clueless, sleeping disciples, a response full of lovingkindness, touches me deeply. No, it blows me away! The question, "So, could you not watch with me one hour?" was not a rebuke so much as a warning. The subsequent words of Jesus make that clear. "Watch and pray that you may not enter into temptation. The spirit indeed is willing, but the flesh is weak."

Jesus had asked the disciples to watch with Him. They failed. Nevertheless, His concern in the face of their indifference was not His own suffering, great as it was. He did not berate them for letting Him down. Instead, He focused on their well-being. "Watch and pray *that you may not enter into temptation.*" Jesus well knew what the disciples were going to face in the coming hours. He had already told Peter plainly that he would deny Him three times before morning. He told all of them that He, the Shepherd, would be struck, and the sheep—the disciples—would

> "So, could you not watch with me one hour?"

be scattered. Jesus knew that they would need to be alert. *Their temptation was the issue, not His.* Jesus knew that Peter would, within a few hours, weep bitter, wracking sobs over his failure. How Jesus, who loved Peter so, longed to spare him that sorrow. *Watch and pray!*

The next words of Jesus were so loving, precious, and poignant that they should have broken the hearts of the sleepy disciples. "The spirit indeed is willing, but the flesh is weak." Instead of highlighting the disciples' weakness and scolding them for it, He commended them for their willing spirit, while acknowledging that He understood that their flesh was not so strong. He acknowledged the internal conflict all believers experience between good intentions and weak performance. *Watch and pray!*

This reminds me of the beautiful words of Psalm 103:13 and 14: "As a father shows compassion to his children, so the LORD shows compassion to those who fear him, for he knows our frame; *he remembers that we are dust."*

The familiar old hymn, *What a Friend We Have in Jesus* contains this similar line, which has comforted saints for generations: "Jesus knows our every weakness, take it to the Lord in prayer."

Jesus poured in the oil and wine. He was ready to forgive. The weakness of the disciples was the very reason He was going to the cross. He would soon make atonement for their sins. Further, He would make a way to rescue them from their weakness. On the basis of His accomplishment of redemption on the cross, He would send His Holy Spirit into the hearts of all believers, so that they would have the power to overcome sin.

What we know of the disciples comes from the book of Acts, where it tells us graphically that they *were* rescued. Their faithfulness and boldness in proclaiming the gospel, in spite of severe persecution, testifies to the accomplishment of Jesus on the cross.

The gifting of the Holy Spirit on the Day of Pentecost began the inward transformation of the disciples, which theologians call *sanctification.*

But there would always be temptations. The prince of evil would never give up, regardless of his defeat. *Watch and pray!*

When Jesus returned for the third time to His sleeping disciples, He was resolute. The real war that took place around Jesus' sacrificial death did not only take place on the cross. It took place in Gethsemane. Evil lost and Jesus won. All the demon armies of hell were routed. Jesus emerged victorious. He would go to the cross and pay for the sins of the world. *"Not as I will. . .your will be done."* The work of Atonement was not finished yet, but it would be.

Poor Peter! He had no idea what he would be facing in the coming hours. He was oblivious to the trouble the near future would bring.

He was also oblivious to his own weakness. How little did he know his own heart. He could never have imagined that a young servant girl would intimidate him to the point of his disowning Jesus.

When Jesus predicted Peter's denial of Him, Peter's answer was an extravagant, "Even if I must die with you, I will not deny you!" (And all the disciples said the same—see Matthew 26:35.)

Overconfidence in self is surely the enemy of watching and praying. Minimizing the lure of temptation is surely the enemy of watching and praying. Underestimating the deceitfulness of the devil (for even Satan disguises himself as an angel of light—see 2 Corinthians 11:14) is surely the enemy of watching and praying. Two Scriptures come to mind:

> Pride goes before destruction, and a haughty spirit before a fall.
> (Proverbs 16:18)

> "Therefore let anyone who thinks that he stands take heed lest he fall."
> (1 Corinthians 10:12)

The latter Scripture is followed by a heap of encouragement.

> No temptation has overtaken you that is uncommon to man. God is faithful and he will not let you be tempted beyond your ability, but with the temptation he will also provide the way of escape that you may be able to endure it.
> (1 Corinthians 10:13)

"So, could you not watch with me one hour?"

Alas, Peter did not take the way of escape.

Be warned with me, dear child of God. The battle for the allegiance of your heart is waged every day. It is waged at home, at school, at the office, on the playground, in the car—wherever our lives take us. There is plenty of danger in this broken world. *Watch and pray!*

Be encouraged as I am, dear child of God. Your lovely and loving Redeemer knows your weakness. His grace will rescue you from you again and again because it is inexhaustible. And as you surrender to His gracious rule, He will gradually make you stronger and stronger, but never so strong that you don't need to. . . *Watch and pray!*

"So, could you not watch with me one hour?"

❖

For Further Thought

Proverbs 4:10–17
Mark 13:32–37
Luke 21:34–36
Ephesians 6:10–18
1 Peter 5:8–11

❖

21

"Woman, why are you weeping?"

JOHN 20:15

Jesus said to her, "Woman, why are you weeping? Whom are you seeking?" Supposing him to be the gardener, she said to him, "Sir, if you have carried him away, tell me where you have laid him, and I will take him away."

You know how you sometimes cry about something, but you're not really crying about that thing. Well, yes, you are crying about that thing, but not *just* about that thing. It's just that it was the "last straw," the final blow. But if it hadn't been for all the other things that had you already terribly sad, maybe you wouldn't have cried so much over *that* thing.

That's what happened to Mary Magdalene on the first "first day of the week," which became the day of the week when Christians around the world would celebrate and worship. She answered the question. The reason for her tears was that the body of Jesus was missing and she didn't know who had taken it, or how to find it. But there was so much more to her tears.

Mary was called "Magdalene" because she came from a rather large village called Magdala on the western coast of the Sea of Galilee. No doubt a fishing village, it was also widely known as a center for the textile industry. It was famous for its dye works, coloring fabric with beautiful hues and artistic designs. Mary Magdalene may even have been associated with the textile industry, because it appears that she was a wealthy woman. How do we know that? Mark 15:40 and 41 state: "There were also women looking on [the crucifixion] from a distance, among whom were Mary Magdalene and Mary the mother of James the younger and of Joses, and Salome. When they were in Galilee, they followed Him and ministered to Him, and there were also many other women who came up with him to Jerusalem." Joanna and Susanna are mentioned in other passages. God used these prominent, well-off women to provide material support to Jesus and His disciples, enabling them to go about their itinerate mission. In order to accomplish this, these women followed Jesus whenever they could.

Many fantastical legends have grown up around Mary Magdalene's memory—from she was a prostitute to she was married to Jesus! These have no basis in fact. There is one very significant fact of Mary Magdalene's life, however, which goes far in explaining her character. She was once demon possessed. In fact, she was possessed of seven demons who tormented her horribly. Most historians believe that her suffering was not physical, but mental and emotional in nature. Anyone who has been tortured in mind and soul knows what great distress Mary Magdalene experienced.

And Jesus healed her! Yes, Jesus cast seven demons from her, and she emerged from that exorcism completely healthy. Is it any wonder that she gave her life to serving Jesus, giving of her considerable means to support Him and the disciples, so that they could do what God had called them to do? Is it any wonder that she came to dearly love her Lord, who had such compassion on her?

As one of Jesus' followers, Mary Magdalene saw the blind receive their sight, saw lepers cleansed, saw the lame walk strongly again. She was most likely acquainted with Mary, Martha, and their brother, Lazarus. She knew about his miraculous resurrection. She heard Jesus' preaching and learned from Him the principles of the kingdom of God.

Those three plus years with Jesus had been amazing. They were full of such grace that, at times, her heart burned within her. At the same time, being the intelligent woman that she was, she well knew that dark clouds were gathering on the horizon. It was plain to see how much the Pharisees and other Jewish leaders hated Jesus. There was even talk that they wanted Him dead.

She would gladly have given her life for Him, but who was she against those men? They had little use for women, anyway, unlike Jesus who treated women with respect and honor. (Even the woman caught in the very act of adultery was gently restored by Jesus, who then shamed her accusers and refused to condemn her. Instead, He empowered her to stop sinning. Mary from Magdala could not forget that scene!)

Sometimes she heard Jesus say strange things about the future, about His death. She didn't want Him to talk like that, and she didn't understand why He would. She believed with all her heart that He was the promised Messiah, and, as such, wouldn't He be a

"Woman, why are you weeping?"

great governor, who would rule over His enemies? He might even deliver Palestine from Roman occupation. But die? He was way too young, had way too much to do to think about death, didn't He? Still, she could sense that His enemies were getting restless.

And then that awful, terrible night happened. It was during the feast of Passover. What should have been a time of celebration and rejoicing in God's deliverance of His people instead became an occasion for murderous bloodlust on the part of Jesus' enemies—no matter that this was supposed to be a religious observance. Jesus was nearby and they had to take advantage of the opportunity to get Him.

Somehow Mary Magdalene heard about Jesus' arrest, and she gathered several of the women together and they found the chaotic crowd and followed along to the residence of Caiaphas the high priest, where He was first interrogated, then on to the governor's headquarters where Pilate questioned Him further.

How it hurt to see Him mistreated. To see and hear Him mocked, abused, humiliated, even tortured, made her sick. It was so unfair. The "witnesses" were such liars! The charges were so phony. The whole thing was a ridiculous setup, but nonetheless dangerous. The crowd was whipped up to a frenzy of outrage and vengeance. Before she could process it all, He was led away to be crucified. She was in shock.

The whole nasty business was expedited because the next day was the Sabbath, and, of course, the angry antagonists could not be held back until the Sabbath was over. Moving along as if in an awful nightmare, Mary Magdalene found herself with the other women at the foot of the cross, observing the unthinkable.

Several hours later, numb, Mary Magdalene joined the other women (who had followed Jesus and His disciples from Galilee to Jerusalem) as they trailed behind Joseph of Arimathea who carried Jesus' body. Joseph donated his own family's tomb, and was given permission from Pilate to inter Jesus' body. Noting where He was entombed, the women returned to their places of residence and prepared ointments and spices with which to anoint His body. (There was no embalming available, so spices and ointments were important to loved ones, who would want the body to be preserved as long as possible.)

They rested on the Sabbath. Rested? Well, they kept the commandments, but their minds were in turmoil and their hearts were broken. Would the sun ever rise again? Would water still boil?

And then it was the first day of the week, and very early—she couldn't sleep anyway—Mary Magdalene went to the tomb with her spices. Upon arriving, she was shocked to find that the stone that had been sealing the tomb had been pushed aside, and the guards were nowhere to be found. She needed reinforcements! She ran to find Simon Peter and John and told them, "They have taken the Lord out of the tomb, and we do not know where they have laid Him" (John 20:2). The three of them ran back to the tomb, where Peter and then John entered, saw the shroud, and confirmed that the body of Jesus was not there. Perplexed, the men returned to their homes, but Mary Magdalene stayed in the garden. She just couldn't bring herself to leave.

This was indeed the final blow to her wounded heart. She loved Him so. If He had to die, she reasoned, then at least she could lovingly care for His body. Now this! It was too much. All the sorrow, shock, and horror of the last forty-eight hours came crashing down on her. And she wept. Did she ever weep! It seemed that there was an endless supply of tears that just kept coming. Still weeping, she stooped down to look inside the tomb and saw two angels who asked her why she was weeping. She answered them with the words she had told Peter and John. "They have taken away my Lord, and I do not know where they have laid Him."

Then she turned around and saw Jesus standing, but didn't recognize Him. He asked the same question:

"Woman, why are you weeping?"

"Sir, if you have carried him away, tell me where you have laid him, and I will take him away." She thought Jesus was the gardener!

Was Mary Magdalene actually weeping over the body being missing? Yes. No. Yes, but not just because the body was missing. All the grief she had stored inside over the last two days came pouring out.

She had to admit to herself that He wasn't the Messiah after

"Woman, why are you weeping?"

all. He claimed to be the Son of the Most High God, and she had believed it! But obviously, He wasn't. Was she a fool? He had healed her for sure. And His preaching! He spoke of the kingdom of God. He spoke of heaven and eternal life. He gave her so much hope. If she had just had a little more time with Him, she would have understood so much more. It was all so confusing. Now all she had was a dead Savior. A dead Messiah. There was a gaping hole in her heart where her hope had been. She didn't think she could go on without Him.

"Woman, why are you weeping?"

Mary Magdalene was weeping because at that moment she had lost eternity. She had lost the promise of life everlasting. The extravagant words of Jesus at the tomb of Lazarus mocked her. "I am the resurrection and the life. Whoever believes in me, though he die, yet shall he live, and everyone who lives and believes in me shall never die" (John 11:25, 26).

Why was she weeping? The answer is in 1 Corinthians 15:14–19: ". . .if Christ has not been raised, then our preaching is in vain and your faith is in vain. . .if Christ has not been raised, your faith is futile and you are still in your sins. . . . If in this life only we have hoped in Christ, we are of all people most to be pitied."

Why was she weeping? She believed Jesus was dead. Period. Yes, it was devastating that His body was gone, but the real tragedy was that her faith and hope were gone. A dead Redeemer is no Redeemer. A dead Rescuer is no Rescuer. She had lost *everything*. She really felt that she would weep for the rest of her life. Without the resurrection, there is nothing. Without the resurrection, Jesus is a fraud, an imposter, a benevolent fantasy character. And real life in this fallen world really *is* broken. Without eternity with Him, there is no present with Him anyway.

And suddenly, immersed in tears, she heard her name. Clearly. And, didn't she recognize that voice? Could she ever forget that voice—the voice that called the demons out of her, the voice that spoke compassion to countless people in need, the voice that forgave sinners—could she ever fail to know that voice?

"Mary." That was *not* the gardener. "Rabboni," she whispered.

Jesus! Teacher! She hadn't known it, but He had been alive the whole day. While she was weeping, He was there. His rhetorical question "Why are you weeping?" was really a statement. "You don't need to weep." Oh, there will be reasons to weep in this troubled world. But you never need to weep over My death or My missing body. "I am with you always, to the end of the age" (Matthew 28:20). "I will never leave you nor forsake you" (Hebrews 13:5).

In Bible college there was a course entitled *Daniel and Revelation* because the two books have a lot in common when it comes to end-time prophecies (which I do not understand). There are two Scriptures, one from each, which are full of gracious encouragement: Easter encouragement, Resurrection hope.

The great deliverance stories of Daniel are very familiar, but one must also note that Daniel suffered a great deal. His life was an incredible saga of heartache and rescue. What is the conclusion? The last verse of the book of Daniel states: "As for you [Daniel], go your way till the end. You will rest, and then at the end of the days you will rise to receive your allotted inheritance" (Daniel 12:13 NIV). Eternity! Daniel will rise again. Faith is forever! Grace is forever!

Revelation 7 is a heart-stopping, breathtaking picture of saints entering heaven—a great multitude from every nation, tribe, people, and language standing before the Lamb. Their robes have been washed and made white in the blood of the Lamb. They are given many glorious promises about their forever future. The final one is this: "And God will wipe away every tear from their eyes" (Revelation 7:17).

"Mary!" For the rest of your earthly life, you will awake in the morning with the risen Christ. You will go to bed each night with your Lord resurrected. You will face the common struggles of daily life with Easter in your heart. And then when finally you enter the pearly gates, God Himself, with His own fingers, will gently wipe every tear that results from the disappointments of earthly life from your eyes. ". . .neither shall there be mourning nor crying nor pain anymore. . ." (Revelation 21:4).

"Woman, why are you weeping?"

❖

"Woman, why are you weeping?"

For Further Thought
....

Nehemiah 8:9–12
Psalm 30:4,5
Isaiah 35:10
1 Corinthians 15:50–58

❖

22

Children, do you have any fish?

JOHN 21:5

Jesus said to them, "Children, do you have any fish?" They answered him, "No."

As day dawned, seven weary disciples sat uncharacteristically silent in Peter's rather large fishing boat. They were discouraged, maybe slightly embarrassed, definitely perplexed. Typically, early in the morning, a fishing boat would be noisy, busy, full of high energy. The only thing harder than catching a large quantity of fish was hauling a large quantity of fish in to shore. It was backbreaking toil. Not this morning.

It was uncanny. They were experienced fishermen. They were skilled at their profession. And they knew that the Sea of Tiberias, otherwise known as Galilee, was teeming with fish. Why had they worked all night for nothing? How had they failed to catch *anything*?

Why had they even gone fishing in the first place? It was Peter's idea; the others just went along. There was little else to do. It was a strange in-between time. Their beloved Master, Jesus, having been horribly killed, had risen from the dead! They had seen Him twice. One of them, Thomas, had been given the invitation to touch the nail holes in His hands and feet and put his hand in the side wound of Jesus. There was no doubt. He was alive and they were amazed and happy about that. But what now? And where was He? They had continued getting together, sometimes sharing a meal, but no one seemed to know what the future would hold. Fishing would relieve the boredom, fill the empty hours, and they could use the money.

But after being with Jesus for more than three years, fishing just wouldn't cut it. Their hearts weren't in it. That still doesn't explain why they caught nothing. They hadn't forgotten how to fish! As they pondered their situation, they heard a voice calling to them,

"Children, do you have any fish?"

"Children" was a term of endearment. "Lads, do you have fish?" They answered truthfully, "No."

Then whoever called to them said, "Cast the net on the right side of the boat, and you will find some." Strange!

They did as He instructed, and then these strong men had to use all their might and energy to haul the net to shore because of the enormous number of fish. Not just a respectable catch of fish. Rather, abundance. That was the clue they needed. "It is the Lord!" John told the others, marveling at His presence.

That's all Peter needed to hear. In a flash, He was out of the boat. He couldn't wait to see the Lord. The boat would be much too slow getting to shore, dragging that bulging net. Swimming or wading was the only way.

How I would love to know the conversation between Peter and Jesus as they waited for the others to arrive. Perhaps Peter helped Jesus with the final preparations for a simple breakfast on the shore. Jesus had a charcoal fire going, and was grilling fish and bread.

Peter helped the other disciples bring the net to shore. A strange detail—we are told that there were 153 fish in all. Did they count them? Or did Jesus in His omniscience just know how many there were? Abundance was Jesus' way. He said, "I have come that [my sheep] may have life, and have it abundantly" (John 10:10). Jesus doesn't just provide. He provides plentifully. Surely the disciples remembered gathering twelve baskets of leftovers after Jesus fed more than five thousand with a little boy's lunch. Significantly, the net was not torn—another miracle.

And then Jesus served them breakfast. Again, the humble servant leader. On one occasion, He had knelt on the floor before them and washed their feet. Now He prepared and served them a meal.

Later, the disciples would ponder the events of that special morning with the Lord. Historians believe that the fishing boat they likely owned was only four feet wide. Surely, if there were no fish on one side, there would be no fish on the other side, and vice versa. Their bait would certainly have attracted fish only four feet away! Anyway, they were knowledgeable fishermen. How could a carpenter know more about fishing than they did? Strange, but they were used to His miracles. He was well able to create fish where none existed! He was, as Peter had confessed, the Christ, the Son of the Living God. He intervened in nature often.

Later they would realize that not only was the large catch of fish providential—that is, divinely planned—but that so, too, was the whole night of futile fishing. God didn't want them to fish anymore. Perhaps if they had been successful that night, they would have been tempted to return to fishing full-time. They remembered Jesus' words when He initially called them to Himself to be His followers. He promised to make them *fishers of men*. Failure is a blessing if it turns us from our own way and sends us on God's errand. In the future they would live by God's provision for them, as they scattered around their world preaching the gospel and planting new churches, really becoming *fishers of men*.

Later, the disciples would remember how Jesus had preceded them at the shore and prepared breakfast for them. He had nothing more important to do that day! He wanted to be with them. He valued their friendship. How could it be when they were so unworthy? That morning He served them so lovingly.

They didn't deserve such lovingkindness. When Jesus was arrested, they got scared. With the exception of John, they all hid. They weren't there for Him when He needed their support. Peter may have denied Him with words, but they also by their absence, their cowardice, denied Him. And they painfully remembered the Garden of Gethsemane. They couldn't stay awake to watch with Him. They had failed Him miserably. And yet that morning on the beach they were objects of such goodness. How could it be? One thing was clear. Fish and bread were not the only items on that breakfast menu. The main item on the menu was *forgiveness*.

Later, they would realize the enormity of the forgiveness they had received. That welcome to breakfast on the beach spoke volumes. They had been unfaithful, but they were forgiven. Jesus, the Lord, was not finished with them. He had a whole new assignment for them. Forgiveness means having another chance. They had been redeemed. God did not reject them because of their unbelief and disloyalty.

Later, they would realize the awful price Jesus had paid for that forgiveness. They came to understand fully that His death, which at the time they had viewed as a horrible tragedy, was really the greatest victory—a victory for them. In that death, Jesus, who was perfect, became their substitute, taking the place of them as sinners, carrying their guilt on His shoulders. In their stead, He experienced the full wrath of God for evil, even to the extent of being separated, agonizingly, from His Father. They could not comprehend how terrible His suffering was. By it, He had accomplished atonement, once and for all time, for all who would trust Him for salvation. It made them long to go into all the world and share this amazing gospel of grace to everyone they could possibly reach!

A seventeenth-century hymn reads this way:

> *Who was the guilty? Who brought this upon You?*
> *It is my treason, Lord, that has undone You.*
> *'Twas I, Lord Jesus, I it was denied You;*
> *I crucified You.*
>
> *For me, dear Jesus, was Your incarnation,*
> *Your mortal sorrow, and Your life's oblation;*
> *Your death of anguish and Your bitter passion,*
> *for my salvation.*
>
> *Therefore, dear Jesus, since I cannot pay You,*
> *I do adore You and will ever pray You.*
> *Think on Your pity and Your love unswerving,*
> *not my deserving.*[7]

Much later Peter would write to dispersed Jewish Christians, "[Christ] himself bore our sins in his body on the tree, that we might die to sin and live to righteousness. By his wounds you have been healed" (1 Peter 2:24) and "For Christ also suffered once for sins, the righteous for the unrighteous, that he might bring us to God..." (1 Peter 3:18).

---

[7] Johann Heermann, *Ah, Holy Jesus, How Hast Thou Offended*

For the disciples and for us, forgiveness is not God overlooking our transgressions because He is kind. Forgiveness is affirming our guilt, but Jesus, having atoned for it, satisfied the wrath of God—and that is justice and mercy all rolled into one.

That forgiveness changed the disciples. And it all started that morning on the beach as they had breakfast with Jesus, their Lord.

"Children, do you have any fish?"

❖

For Further Thought

Psalm 86:5

Psalm 130:3–8

Romans 5:6–11

❖

23

"Do you love me?"

JOHN 21:16

He said to him a second time, "Simon, son of John, do you love me?" He said to him, "Yes, Lord; you know that I love you." He said to him, "Tend my sheep."

It was, hands down, the worst night of his life. What he would give to have a do-over of that awful time! He had believed himself devoted to Jesus, strong in faith, invulnerable to any temptation to disloyalty. But he had failed spectacularly. Jesus had predicted his cowardice, his lies, his treason. He hadn't believed it. He was way overconfident.

When the cock crowed, signaling the fulfillment of Jesus' prediction, Peter fell apart. Heart pounding, breathing difficult, he remembered the three occasions within a short period of time when he denied being in any way associated with Jesus. What a joke he was! The tears came quickly and hard. His whole body wracked with sobs, chest heaving, he cried until there were no more tears.

He could never face Jesus again. Never. But, oh, how he wanted to! He could hardly comprehend how much Jesus was suffering. And he had added to that travail by his abandonment of Him. Jesus would be so disappointed in him. They had certainly had a special relationship, he and Jesus. But after this, Jesus wouldn't want to see him anymore. Could that special friendship *really* be over? He was so sorry for his fear-filled treachery. Would there ever be a possibility of conveying to Jesus his sorrow and regret?

It seemed that his life was over. However, Jesus *had* promised to make him a *fisher of men*.

Jesus had revealed Himself to be the light of the world, the bread of life, the Good Shepherd, the eternal Word, the living water, the Christ, the Son of the Living God. How could he live without Him? When Jesus once asked the disciples if they wanted to go away from Him, Peter was the one who responded, "To whom shall we go? You have the words of eternal life" (John 6:68).

Anyway, Jesus was dead. Yes, His enemies had succeeded in convicting and crucifying Him. Unworthy, he, Peter, had stayed away, although he couldn't help but monitor events from a distance. Would there never be an opportunity to tell Him he was so sorry? Would there never be an opportunity to try to make amends?

The other disciples, minus Judas who had killed himself after his betrayal of Jesus, accepted Peter into their company that Sabbath day. It was embarrassing at first to face them, but he couldn't stay away. Being with the disciples seemed to be the closest he could get to Jesus. And he desperately wanted to hear more of what had taken place over the last twenty-four hours. They didn't know much, however, because they, too, were scared and stayed away from the whole horrifying mess.

Early Sunday morning there was a loud, insistent knocking on his door. It was *really* early. His defeat and discouragement made him slightly depressed, and it had been hard to sleep. Groggily, he answered the door, and was shocked to see some women—women he knew who had followed Jesus and provided a lot of material support for Him and the disciples. "Jesus has risen! He is alive!" they cried, excited, faces beaming. Then they said something Peter would never forget, "He said, 'But go, tell his disciples *and Peter* that He is going before you to Galilee. There you will see him" (Mark 16:7).

Peter would never ever forget those two words, "and Peter." Mark is the only Gospel writer who recorded those two little words. Mark was not one of the disciples. Historical tradition holds that his Gospel account was likely dictated by *Peter*. No wonder Mark included those words! They were deeply engraved on Peter's heart.

Did Jesus and Peter meet privately during those early days after the resurrection? The Gospels do not record such a meeting, but it likely took place. Peter wanted to repent, and Jesus wanted to forgive and restore Peter. If such a meeting did take place, Peter would have fallen on his face at Jesus' feet, poignantly expressing his painful regret, and begging for forgiveness. Jesus would have stooped down and raised Peter to his feet, embracing him and assuring him of love and acceptance. There is no way to adequately describe that emotional meeting.

And then came the day when, early in the morning, Jesus prepared breakfast on a Galilean beach.

The disciples and Jesus were relaxed on the sand, having

"Do you love me?"

finished eating, when Jesus turned to Peter,

"Simon, son of John, do you love me more than these?"

What a question! It must have caused Peter's heart to beat faster.

The use of Peter's full formal name speaks to the seriousness of the question. One's formal name is used on significant documents, in courts of law, in solemn proceedings. Most of us can remember the use of our full names by our mothers signifying that we were in trouble! For Peter, hearing his formal name meant that this was suddenly a consequential occasion, a sobering question.

Why did Jesus ask such a personal question publicly—that is, in front of the other disciples? Jesus was giving Peter an opportunity to affirm his repentance in front of the others. There is an old axiom: *private sin, private repentance; public sin, public repentance.* Peter had denied Jesus out loud in a public place. The other disciples knew of it. Three denials, now three affirmations of love. In the future, Peter was to be not just a friend, but a colleague in the formation of the early church. He would become a leader, and a writer of two inspired books of the New Testament. All the disciples would need to respect him as such.

Repentance means to do a one-eighty—that is, to completely change direction: turn around and go the other way. It means to turn *from* one's own way, but that is only the first part. It is equally important to turn *to* the Lord, to go His way. *"Do you love me?"*

Once again, focus is placed on the *heart*. Jesus did not question Peter about his future plans. Jesus asked him about his heart. The essence of sin is self-centeredness. Transforming grace redirects our hearts from love of self to love of God.

Love for God comes *before* service to Christ. Love for God is the foundation for worship and service of Christ. Sadly, it is all too possible to do acts of service from selfish motivations, but love is the pure motivation for serving Christ. Love is more important than what one does. Love determines the quality of what one does.

This probing question "Do you love me?" exposed Peter's heart, but it also exposed Jesus' heart. One doesn't ask this question of another person unless one loves that person! Otherwise, who cares? Jesus deeply loved Peter, so He asked this poignant question, "Do you love me?" Can you hear the longing of His heart in those words?

". . .more than these. . ."

This phrase called Peter back to some fateful words of his, spoken on the night Jesus was betrayed and arrested. At the Mount of Olives, Jesus said to the disciples, "You will all fall away; for it is written, 'I will strike the shepherd, and the sheep will be scattered.'" to which Peter replied, "Even though they all fall away, I will not" (Mark 14:27–29).

Peter, with self-righteous confidence, professed himself better than the other disciples! Now, humbled after his dramatic failure, he was asked if he still considered that he loved Jesus more than the others did, "Do you love me *more than these?*" A chastened Peter would never again profess that his love for Jesus was greater than the love of others for Jesus. He got it. He simply answered, *"Yes, Lord, you know that I love you."* Indeed, Jesus did know it.

Each time Peter affirmed his love, Jesus instructed him to feed His people. The first time, He said, "Feed my lambs," my baby sheep. We see it as a term of endearment in Isaiah 40:11, "[The Lord God] will tend his flock like a shepherd; he will g*ather the lambs in his arms*; he will carry them in his bosom. . ." God's love is conferred most caringly on the vulnerable. The other two times, Jesus said to Peter, "Feed my sheep."

Throughout the Bible, Psalm 23 being the best-known example, God in Christ is presented as a Shepherd, and His chosen people as His sheep. It is an eloquent and tender metaphor. From this point on in the New Testament, spiritual leaders such as elders and pastors are said to be shepherds who are tasked with the responsibility of caring for the people of God. Paul addressed the Ephesian elders in Acts 20:28, "Pay careful attention to yourselves and to all the flock, in which the Holy Spirit has made you overseers, to care for the church of God, which he obtained with his own blood." "Flock" is synonymous with herd of sheep. Peter himself would later write to the dispersed believers throughout Asia minor, "So I exhort the elders among you. . .shepherd the flock of God that is among you" (1 Peter 5:1,2).

Jesus was assigning Peter the role of shepherd of His people, His lambs, His sheep. It was a solemn charge.

"Peter was grieved because [Jesus] said to him the third time, 'Do you love me?'" In this third question, Peter heard again the

"Do you love me?"

cock crowing. He felt again the pain of his unfaithfulness to his Lord, whom he *did* truly love. Forgiveness takes away the guilt and pollution of sin. It does not erase the memory, which can serve to keep one humble. *Watch and pray!*

A nineteenth-century hymn gives voice to my soul's petition:

> *More love to Thee, O Christ, more love to Thee!*
> *Hear Thou the prayer I make on bended knee;*
> *This is my earnest plea, more love, O Christ to Thee.*
>
> *Then shall my latest breath whisper Thy praise;*
> *This be the parting cry my heart shall raise,*
> *This still its prayer shall be, more love, O Christ to Thee.*[8]

Jesus continued with Peter, predicting his death by crucifixion. Formerly, Peter had arrogantly proclaimed, "Even if I must die with you, I will not deny you!" (Matthew 26:35). A different Peter here on the beach simply accepted the cost that would be involved in fulfilling Jesus' assignment for him. A different Peter—repentant, forgiven, restored, inspired.

The scene closes with the same words that began Jesus' relationship with Peter:

> While walking by the Sea of Galilee, [Jesus] saw two brothers, Simon (who is called Peter) and Andrew his brother, casting a net into the sea, for they were fishermen. And he said to them "Follow me. . . ."
> (Matthew 4:18)

After showing Peter by what kind of death he was to glorify God, Jesus said, *"Follow me."* Those two common words say it all. They embody what it means to love Jesus. Love is the heart. Following is the enterprise.

> *"Do you love me?*

❖

[8] Elizabeth Payson Prentiss, *More Love to Thee*

For Further Thought

Exodus 20:1–6
Deuteronomy 6:4,5
1 Corinthians 13:1–13
1 Peter 1:8–9
1 John 4:19

❖

"Do you love me?"

24

"Saul, Saul, why are you persecuting me?"

ACTS 9:4

And falling to the ground, he heard a voice saying to him, "Saul, Saul, why are you persecuting me?"

This Jesus cult, also known as the sect of the Nazarene, or for short *the Way*, (referring to Jesus' statement that He is the Way, the Truth, and the Life), was becoming an even bigger problem. Make it too difficult for these people in one locale, and they either went underground or they migrated to another place and spread their poisonous message there. For example: They fled Jerusalem where they had been severely persecuted, and as a result their Jesus message echoed all over the Middle East.

Saul was a man to be reckoned with, an impressive adversary. He described himself as "Circumcised on the eighth day of the people of Israel, of the tribe of Benjamin, a Hebrew of Hebrews; as to the law, a Pharisee, as to zeal, a persecutor of the church; as to righteousness under the law blameless" (Philippians 3:5,6). Educated in Jewish law under the eminent Gamaliel, he was highly respected. And he was incensed.

Just recently, that Jesus man, Stephen, preached a long open-air sermon that, as far as he was concerned, totally disrespected Jewish religion and history and insulted Jews everywhere. It was a distortion and a disgrace. Saul was so outraged by it that he gladly witnessed the stoning of Stephen. He even kept watch over the outer garments of Stephen's attackers. He himself didn't throw any stones. That wasn't his style. Trained in the law, he worked the system.

He was able to get injunctions against the people of the Way. Using the law could rid a fairly large area of the whole lot of them. Stoning was too messy and much too slow. Saul had no time to deal with them one at a time. While it was true that the high priests had no real legal authority, they had unchallenged ecclesiastical authority and could exert enormous pressure on local synagogue leaders. It worked like a charm. Using letters from the Jerusalem high priests, Saul could have Jesus people, a whole group of them together, arrested. They could rot in jail. Eventually, those who survived captivity would be taken to Jerusalem to stand trial and be executed. It was Saul's mission. Hatred is not too strong a word to describe his feelings for Jesus' followers. He was intense, driven, and determined in his goal.

And then one day, in a stunning display of sovereign grace, Saul himself was arrested! It happened like this: Damascus, the capital of Syria, and an important cultural and commercial center, was the destination. A large group of believers in Jesus had migrated there. Saul had received letters from the high priests in Jerusalem to the synagogue leaders in Damascus authorizing him to arrest any and all who belonged to the Way, men or women, and take them, bound, back to Jerusalem to await trial and penalty.

Damascus was approximately 140 miles northeast of Jerusalem. It would take about a week to travel there on foot. Saul had an entourage with him, made up of police officers, officers of the temple, as well as nomads, groupies, and hangers-on, who, like fire engine chasers, fed off the thrill of human tragedy.

It was midday, but the sun was hardly the only source of heat. Saul himself was so worked up that it seemed every breath he exhaled was hot with murderous rage. He was impatient to get on with his mission, and the journey was taking way too long.

Suddenly, when his long trek was about to end, as he was approaching Damascus, a brilliant light, far brighter than the sun, brighter than any light known in nature, shone around him. It was so resplendent that it temporarily blinded him. Throughout Scripture, whenever God appeared, He was enclosed in radiance. Jewish rabbis coined a word for it—*shekinah glory*. It happened on Mount Sinai during the giving of the ten commandments, it happened when the angels appeared to the shepherds announcing Christ's birth, and it happened on the Mount of Transfiguration, to mention only a few of its occurrences. *And it happened here!*

The shekinah glory was impossible to ignore. Saul immediately fell to the ground and then he heard a voice speaking out of the glory,

> *"Saul, Saul, why are you persecuting me?"*

The brilliant radiance coupled with the double use of his name got Saul's attention all right!

"Why are you persecuting me?" The word "me" gives a whole new dimension to Saul's situation. He didn't at all consider himself persecuting *God,* or even Jesus, whom he considered dead. In his mind, he was persecuting misguided people who were upsetting the faith and culture of the Jewish nation, doing injury to the history and traditions of which he was so proud. God saw it differently. He identified with His people. "Truly, I say to you, as you did it to one of the least of these my brothers, you did it to me." (These are the words of Jesus in Matthew 25:40.) Persecuting believers in Jesus *was* persecuting Jesus Himself.

"Why?" For Saul, Jesus was an enormous threat to his whole belief system. He hated the words of Jesus when He said things like, "You have heard that it was said of old. . . but I say to you." How could Jesus contradict the Torah? How could Jesus challenge the Pharisees, calling them whitewashed sepulchers full of dead men's bones, or filthy cups clean on the outside only, or vipers?

Jesus' person, work, and teaching, continuing on in the people who loved and followed Him, threatened the whole Old Testament culture embodied in the law and the prophets. Saul was deeply invested in that culture. He had chosen a path of strict adherence to ecclesiastical law. He was highly educated and practiced in Jewish tradition; it was his life's blood.

Christianity was always meant to replace Old Testament Judaism, because the person and work of Jesus was the *fulfillment* of Judaism's promises, beginning with the promise to Eve in the Garden of Eden that from her progeny would come a Savior to defeat the devil and his evil works. Not just the prophecies, but all the Old Testament teachings and traditions were established by God to prepare for, and introduce, Jesus the Messiah.

For example, all of Israel heard or read the prophets. Hebrews 1:1,2 asserts, "Long ago, at many times and in many ways, God spoke to our fathers by the prophets, but in these last days he has spoken to us by his Son."

All of Israel interacted with priests who represented them before God. Hebrews 4:14 announces, "Since then we have a great high priest who has passed through the heavens, Jesus, the Son of God, let us hold fast our confession."

All Jewish people were familiar with the idea of a king. They looked back proudly on the reigns of David and Solomon, when their nation was at its height of power and beauty. In Matthew 2:2, the wise men came to Jerusalem asking, "Where is he who has been born king of the Jews? For we saw his star when it rose and have come to worship him." In a stunning irony, Pilate got it right when he posted a sign on the cross announcing that the crucified was "King of the Jews."

For centuries and generations, Hebrews had been offering perfect *lambs* as sacrificial substitutes to be killed for their sins. John the Baptist introduced Jesus this way: "Behold, the Lamb of God, who takes away the sin of the world!" (John 1:29).

"Why?" There is a simpler yet more profound answer to that question. The best answer to that question was Saul's response to the voice out of the shekinah glory. Having fallen to the ground, Saul asked, "Who are you, Lord?" This proud, entitled elitist was humbled! He was on the ground, he was blind, and he had to admit he didn't know who was talking to him. *"Lord"* was a commonsense appellation, given the radiance, but Saul didn't know who He was.

The bottom-line reason Saul was persecuting Jesus' followers? He didn't know who Jesus was! He knew a lot of theology. He knew Jewish law. He knew history and tradition. *He didn't know Jesus.* He had been persecuting his own fantasy, his own opinion, his interpretation of all the rumors about the Nazarene teacher. *He didn't know Jesus.*

Saul hadn't partaken of the water made into the finest wine. He hadn't been in the boat when Jesus calmed the raging storm with three little words: *"Peace, be still."* He hadn't seen Jesus actually *touch* the leper. He hadn't witnessed Jesus' loving dealings with the woman who had a bleeding disorder. He wasn't present when Lazarus was raised from the dead, or when more than five thousand people where fed from a boy's small lunch.

He didn't know about Jesus' compassion on the woman caught in adultery. His sandy, smelly feet had not been washed by a kneeling Jesus dressed as a servant. He wasn't around when Jesus reached up and healed the bleeding ear of a soldier trying to arrest Him. He knew nothing of Jesus' lovingkindness to Peter, who had denied Him, not once, but three times! Saul had never tasted such forgiveness. Sadly, Saul did not walk with the three on the road to Emmaus and hear Jesus expound all the Old Testament Scriptures *concerning Himself.*

Saul hadn't spoken with the risen Jesus, or watched Him ascend into heaven. *Saul didn't know Jesus.*

In one of the clearest interventions of sovereign grace, all that was about to change!

> And the Lord said, "I am Jesus whom you are persecuting. But rise and stand upon your feet for I have appeared to you for this purpose, to appoint you as a servant and witness to the things in which you have seen me and to those in which I will appear to you, delivering you from your people and from the Gentiles—to whom I am sending you to open their eyes, so that they may turn from darkness to light and from the power of Satan to God, that they may receive forgiveness of sins and a place among those who are sanctified by faith in me."
> (Acts 26:15–18)

In the immediate interim, God used a precious saint named Ananias to nurture Saul in the gospel. The Lord said to Ananias, ". . . he is a chosen instrument of mine to carry my name before Gentiles and kings and the children of Israel" (Acts 9:15), echoing Jesus' words to Saul while he was still prostrate on the ground.

Saul's transformation was so complete that even his name was changed. He became Paul and ended up writing most of the New Testament Scriptures! This very day, all over the world, Paul's inspired words are being read and studied!

Consder Paul's testimony to the Philippian church:

> If anyone else thinks he has reason for confidence in the flesh, I have more. . . . But whatever gain I had, I counted as loss for the sake of Christ. Indeed, I count everything as loss because of the surpassing worth of knowing

Christ Jesus my Lord. For his sake I have suffered the loss of all things and count them as rubbish, in order that I may gain Christ and be found in him, not having a righteousness of my own that comes from the law, but that which comes through faith in Christ, the righteousness from God that depends on faith—that I may know him and the power of his resurrection and may share his sufferings becoming like him in death, that by any means possible I may attain the resurrection from the dead. (Philippians 3:4–11)

Consider the words of an old missionary, written to his protégé Timothy, as he, Paul, awaited execution in a Roman jail. "But I am not ashamed, for I know whom I have believed, and I am convinced that he is able to guard until that Day what has been entrusted to me" (2 Timothy 1:12). And, "But the Lord stood by me and strengthened me, so that through me the message might be fully proclaimed and all the Gentiles might hear it. So I was rescued from the lion's mouth. The Lord will rescue me from every evil deed and bring me safely into his heavenly kingdom. To him be the glory forever and ever. Amen" (2 Timothy 4:17,18).

"Saul, Saul, why are you persecuting me?"

❖

"Saul, Saul, why are you persecuting me?"

For Further Thought

Ephesians 1:15–23
Ephesians 2:11–22
Ephesians 3:14–21
Philippians 1:21

❖

Conclusion

As I conclude this study of God's questions, I am reminded of the title of an important book by Francis Schaeffer, a Christian philosopher and apologist of the last century: *He Is There and He Is Not Silent*.

The very character of God, and the fact of His creation of man, ensures that He communicates with the men and women He has made. We were made for Him, and for His glory, so it follows that He would want us to know Him, and therefore He would want to reveal to us His person and His work. *He cannot be silent!* Thus, Holy Scripture.

Chesed is the Hebrew word that over and over in the Old Testament is used to describe the character of God. *Chesed* means *lovingkindness*. Psalm 136 highlights this disposition of God, as it explains Israel's history in terms of the frequent refrain, "for His steadfast love endures forever." Steadfast love, *chesed*.

God's lovingkindness motivates His communication to men and women both in nature and in His foremost communication, His Word, the Bible, a treasure of the knowledge of God. *He is not silent.*

One can communicate in a variety of ways. Many of them involve the speaker alone, such as when one lectures, instructs, explains, or commands. The object of the communication may or may not be listening or responding. A question, however, is unique in that it necessarily involves the other person. A question is a demanding form of communication, in that it expects an *answer* from the other person. Questions assume, even insist upon, *two-way* communication.

That makes questions a powerful form of discourse, and in the case of *God's* questions, it is a special manifestation of God's grace toward sinners—*chesed*. God wants to *interact* with His creatures, and He makes sure He gets their attention!

If the very existence of God's questions is evidence of His love and faithfulness—*chesed*—so also the *content* of His questions. It is gracious, as we have seen in the study that is this book. God's questions are pointed and practical. God's questions awaken the other person from vague thoughts or denial of reality, so that He can effect a rescue of him in redeeming love.

Adam, where are you? Moses, what do you have in your hand? Elijah, what are you doing here? Simon, do you see this woman? Why are you so afraid? Mary, why are you crying?

Scripture is eternal, yet amazingly contemporary, though written thousands of years ago. I trust the questions we have perused in this book have been instructive for you. I hope they have encouraged you in your own personal pursuit of God.

God still asks questions today. If you have not yet heard one, stay tuned to Him. God may ask *you* a pointed question. Though it may be an uncomfortable question, it is a measure of His love for you, and His desire to interact with you in love and grace, for His glory and for your eternal good.

❖

Afterword:
Did you mean it?

Long before even a hint of the idea for this book came to mind, God asked *me* a question. I was sitting in a rocker in the living room of my hundred-year-old-being-renovated house, trying to settle my very fussy infant son, while my two-year-old daughter played with some toys at my feet. It was taking some time, and as I rocked, I was thinking sad thoughts.

My life wasn't exactly turning out the way I had planned. Instead, all my ambitions, hopes, dreams, and plans were pretty much crushed. While I was surely committed to my marriage, my husband's serial infidelity hurt my heart and made our future insecure. I prayed mightily that God would work a miracle, and tried to hope and believe for it, but I had to admit that, at the present, there was no evidence of that miracle.

"Did you mean it?"

That was the question. It came strongly to mind as I rocked. And just as strongly came the realization that God was speaking to me. And just as strongly, I knew exactly what He was referring to.

Several years earlier, when I was a senior in Bible College, and during a week of special meetings headlined by a famous evangelist, I wrote a poem on one of the blank white pages in my Bible. It was during the last of the meetings, and the theme was surrendering to God's will for one's life—that is, seeking to know God's wisdom in choosing one's future path, and obeying His direction. The preaching ended with this poem, which was a prayer, and in which a series of options was affirmed. *"I am willing to go here for You; I am willing to go there for You. . . I am willing to do this for You; I am willing to do that for You. . .I am willing to be this; I am willing to be that. . .* And then the last line: *"I am willing to be nothing for You."*

Of course, it was understood that *nothing* didn't mean a zero. It meant *nothing that would be considered newsworthy, nothing famous, nothing drawing attention. Nothing that the society would value.*

I was so touched by that preaching, and the poem, that instead of going back to my dorm room after the meeting was dismissed, I went to the prayer room provided in my dormitory for use when one wanted to be alone. I prayed that poem and prayer with all sincerity, tears streaming down my face. *I am willing to be nothing for You.* Yes, I said it.

This day, in my disorganized farmhouse in a rural community, I got up from my rocking chair and went to the bookcase and pulled out that Bible I had carried in college, and read the poem again.

"Did you mean it?"

I am willing to be nothing for You. Nothing was obviously the operative word. Really? Now, I was a very ambitious young woman.

I remonstrated, (sigh), *but I wasn't going to be nothing. . .I was going to be a great missionary. I was going to be the kind of missionary about whom books are written!* Ever since I was a teenager, I had immersed myself in everything missionary. My husband had to agree to be a missionary before I would accept his marriage proposal. Alas!

But truth—here I was in my remote unfinished farmhouse, anonymous wife of a carpenter (who had a serious problem), mother of two preschoolers. For sure I wasn't going to be a missionary—not that I could imagine. This day it came down on me like a smothering avalanche. My life's ambition, my grand dream, was in shambles.

Did I mean it? After a while the fight went out of me, and I admitted to God what I knew to be the truth. *I meant it.*

And I knew that for me that meant settling down to being a housewife—*only.* Oh, I suppose I could have pursued another career, but I had a strong sense that motherhood was job one for me.

You have to know that the year was 1972. It was near the dawning of what was then called *The Women's Liberation Movement.* Most women in prior generations spent their lives as homemakers.

Afterword: Did you mean it?

They spent their days nurturing their husbands and children. But now, women in the droves were abandoning that role to have careers, or at least jobs. It was all over the media. You couldn't pick up a popular magazine without this novel movement being touted as giving women new freedom and dignity. Housewives were *not* honored. To be a homemaker in 1972 was to be. . .well, *nothing*.

God challenged me that day. Could I wash dishes for Jesus? Could I change dirty diapers for Jesus? Could I clean house for Jesus? *For Jesus*—that made all the difference. *For Jesus* elevated the most menial task into something lofty and grand, even eternal! *The hand that rocks the cradle rules the world*—could that be so? Well, the hand that is guided by the Sovereign Savior does truly significant work.

So for the next twenty years, I did what women everywhere have done through the ages—20,000 loads of laundry, 60,000 plus meals prepared, 10,000 grocery shopping trips, and so much more.

And then, finally, divorce. Not the outcome I longed for, but it was inevitable. It was not pretty.

In my brokenness and grief, I realized one day that now I could be a missionary. My children were almost entirely grown up, I was free from the bonds of marriage, and *I could do this!* It was a good thought.

It was an absurd thought. I was much too old to be considered a career missionary, and I wasn't particularly interested in *short-term* missions. And I was divorced! In most non-western countries, divorce is much less acceptable than it is in the U.S., especially in Christian circles. And, really, I was a mess. My finances were a mess, my children were a mess, and my heart was a mess. I was beginning to go to counseling to try to make sense of the detritus of my life. A missionary? What was I thinking?

But wait, it *was* a good thought, a thought worth hanging on to. I began to share my shaky vision with some close friends and mentors. I even wrote to a longtime family friend in India (my ex-husband was a "missionary kid" from India, born and raised there) to see if there might be something useful for me to do there—or was I just foolish? Everyone, to a person, encouraged me to pursue my dream.

The next thing I did was to begin learning Tamil, the language of South India, and which I never mastered—there are 247 letters in the alphabet!

It took me seven years to get my life in order—to see my children safely into adulthood, to get out of debt, to raise money for my missionary endeavor, and, most of all, to find rescue and healing for my soul. But after seven years, on a warm June day, I boarded a plane for South Asia. God was giving me the desire of my heart!

I spent just under eight years in South India, teaching piano and English in a small Bible college. They may have been the happiest years of my life, and I only left because by then I had several precious grandchildren whom I wanted to know.

Sometimes words of devotion to God too easily roll off our lips, and God then challenges us.

"Did you mean it?"

❖

BarbaraJo Tripp Bowers has a B.A. in Bible from Columbia International University in South Carolina. For several years she taught piano, worship music, and English at a Bible College in India. She now resides in Illinois with her husband, George, where she enjoys teaching piano, gardening, and especially being a grandmother.

About Shepherd Press Publications

They are gospel driven.
They are heart focused.
They are life changing.

Our Invitation to You

We passionately believe that what we are publishing can be of benefit to you, your family, your friends, and your work colleagues. So we are inviting you to join our online mailing list so that we may reach out to you with news about our latest and forthcoming publications, and with special offers.

Visit:

www.shepherdpress.com/newsletter

and provide your name and email address.